Larry,
I will miss talking
golf with you- I know
your retirement will be
wonderful and no
" rough stuff" along the
way- Enjoy!,
d Sarah

Rough Stuff

THE GOLF COLUMNS OF DENNIS McCANN

Published originally in *Wisconsin Golfer* magazine

Killarney
GOLF MEDIA

Madison, Wisconsin

To Barb, and to all those lonely shepherds
who gave us this wonderful game.

Published by
Killarney Golf Media Inc.
P.O. Box 14439
Madison, WI 53708-0439
www.wisgolfer.com

Illustrations by Heather Martin of Calluna Graphic Design
Cover design by Ali Head of Dunlop Associates, Inc.
Cover photography by Rick Pledl

2007929761

Printed in the U.S.A.

ISBN 978-0-9796931-0-6

CONTENTS

FOREWORD

Bob Hope is in the World Golf Hall of Fame, but never won an Oscar. Jack Lemmon won two Oscars, but never made the cut in the old Crosby Clambake. (Remember the classic Phil Harris line: "Jack Lemmon has been in more bunkers than Eva Braun"?)

No one gets everything they desire, I guess.

Another case in point: Dennis McCann has had a successful career in Wisconsin as an author and longtime columnist for the state's largest newspaper, the *Milwaukee Journal Sentinel*. He writes with wit, sensitivity and not a small measure of humor – often in the same piece. But, alas, on the golf course he has never broken 80.

Not for lack of trying. In his quest, McCann has prowled the links of Wisconsin from Bayfield to South Milwaukee, from the first rays of dewy morning on into the gloaming, when mosquitoes claim their turf. A cynic – or realist – might suggest that as the years pass, McCann's chances of finishing a round with a score on the pro side of 80 diminish, if even ever so slightly.

Our author, however, always the optimist, takes a different view. As the years add up, he reasons, he draws ever closer to that other eternal goal in golf – that of shooting his age.

As readers of his work, it really matters little to us if McCann ever reaches either of his elusive goals in golf. In fact, it probably adds to his charm if he doesn't – like Charlie Brown and his never-ending quest to kick that damn football.

What's important to us is that McCann continues his sub-par work as a writer. (That doesn't sound quite right, I know, but given that we are all golf enthusiasts here, I think you know what I mean.)

I first met McCann when we both worked at the *Janesville Gazette*, um, quite a few years ago. We moved on, then reconnected when he agreed to pen a column for our magazine, *Wisconsin Golf*, later to become *Wisconsin Golfer*. Happily, he continues in that role to this day, almost 15 years later. I can assure you he's not doing it for the money, but rather, it must be, for the love of his craft and for the game that brings him into contact with so many interesting people.

This compilation of McCann's columns from *Wisconsin Golf/Wisconsin Golfer* probably is long overdue. We don't bill it as "the best of" Dennis McCann, because, frankly, everything he has done for the magazine has been absolutely first-rate. It is, therefore, merely a sampling of his fine work throughout the years.

I hope McCann breaks 80 before he passes on, as he puts it, "to that back nine that never ends." But if he doesn't, no matter. His real gift is an ability to arrange words on a page in a manner that evokes emotions from his readers. And, like Tiger Woods striping a 1-iron 280 yards, he makes it look easy.

Enjoy "Rough Stuff."

– John Hughes, Publisher

Digging around (figuratively) for the grave of Bobby Jones

May 2003

Grave matters today, friends. There I was one recent day in an old cemetery in Atlanta, searching for the headstone of ...

Wait, you're saying, what's up with that? What does a boneyard in Atlanta have to do with Wisconsin golf? Haven't you looked at your magazine's title lately?

Well, yes, I have, and I can connect the plots. In a couple of hours I would be leaving for my home in Wisconsin, but not until I found a certain grave, the final resting place of one Robert Tyre Jones.

Bobby, to his friends. Let Janis Joplin sing of Bobby McGee. This was about Bobby and me.

It started a few years ago when some friends and I were in Augusta, browsing a display of golf memorabilia. One item was a piece of paper – a check, maybe, or a receipt – signed by none other than the greatest amateur golfer ever, and it included his address. So the next day, back in Atlanta, we drove around the tony Buckhead district for several hours looking for Bobby's house.

Not that he owned it anymore, of course, and I don't know what we would have done if we had found it. Perhaps we would have posed for a hokey photo, the way we did one inky morning outside of Eastlake GC, Jones' home course in Atlanta. It was so early that the resulting picture showed three mopes with crazy grins in front of a background so dark we could have been outside Janesville Riverside GC at midnight.

We never found the house, though, in large part because the address had Peachtree in it somewhere and Atlanta has some 50 streets, avenues, boulevards, lanes using some form of Peachtree – and that's before you begin adding directionals. It is not uncommon to find the intersection of, say, Northeast Peachtree Street and Southwest Peachtree Boulevard. just up the street from Northwest Peachtree Lane. How confounding. I bet there are Atlantans who buy a new house, go to work the first day and never see their families again.

But having failed to find where Bobby Jones spent his adult life, I knew I could find where he was spending the back nine that never ends. I was in Atlanta with Dale, a photographer, on important newspaper business – yes, there is such a thing – when I found a brochure for historic Oakland Cemetery, where among many other wondrous burial sites was Bobby Jones' grave. Dale, I said, this we have to see.

He looked at me like the fever had finally taken my mind, which is what I get for traveling with a nongolfer. The first day he just laughed, like I was kidding, but when I kept mentioning the cemetery and what a shame it would be to miss it, he began to think I was serious. Finally, with a few hours to kill before our flight home, he allowed as how Oakland Cemetery might be on the way to the airport and maybe we could swing in.

Well, what could be better? I love old boneyards anyway, and this was as much a tourist must-see as about anything in Atlanta. It was founded in 1850, has 70,000 (very quiet) residents and is listed on the National Register of Historic Places for its significant Victorian funerary sculpture and for the many once-important Georgians who are buried there.

There are nearly 6,900 soldiers in the Confederate Section who died during fighting in and around Atlanta, and another 3,000 unknown Confederates nearby, guarded by a massive statue of a dying lion resting on a Confederate flag. (In the back row there are also 16 Union soldiers who must ask themselves daily where they went wrong.) Margaret Mitchell, of "Gone With the Wind" fame, is there. There is a Black Section, set aside in post-war years for former slaves, a Jewish Section, a Potter's Field with 17,000 unmarked graves, even a grave for Tweet the Mockingbird, one of several pets buried there. Some of the mausoleums were as big as my first house.

I enjoyed them all, but they were mere diversions on the way to the grave of the greatest amateur golfer ever. He and his wife, Mary Malone Jones, are buried along a red brick fence in a setting that can only be called just right. The grass in front of the headstone is mowed short and shaped like a putting green. Around the gravesite are 18 specimens of plants, one from each of the holes at Augusta National GC. And on the short grass were several golf balls left by visitors.

That's my one regret. I was happy to find the spot, but no one had told me it was something of a tradition for a visiting golfer to leave a ball behind, both to honor the memory of Bobby Jones and to bring good luck to the visitor's game. I didn't have a ball to leave, so if the legend is also true in reverse my game will surely go to hell for my failure.

I would have gone to buy a sleeve nearby if I hadn't feared Dale would head for the airport without me. The man just had no respect for the dead. While I was paying my respects, he stood skeptically and said, "Look at that. Instead of a hole-in-one, he's the one in a hole."

He didn't want to eat across the street in the diner called Six Feet Under. And he declined my offer on the way out to stop at Margaret Mitchell's grave.

"Frankly," he said, "I don't give a damn."

Author's Note: On another trip to Biloxi, I introduced Dale to two of life's three top vices – golf and gambling. Sadly, Dale died of a heart attack in 2005 at an early age. I think of him often, and fondly.

Fawning over
a battered Bambi

July 2004

This one moved me to tears, then to song. Or a variation, anyway: "Doh! a deer ... "

Matt Buettell was working with the grounds crew at Eagle River GC one day last spring, edging sand traps and the like on the 10th fairway, when they saw a single approach the tee. Having served as the unwitting targets of errant golfers in the past, they looked up from their labor to watch the shot.

"He whaled on it," Buettell recalled. "He – what's the one that goes to the right, a slice or a hook – he sliced a real nice one. It went right into a tree."

Or did it?

"It made a strange noise," Buettell said, not the sharp doink he might have expected to hear. "It didn't sound like a golf ball hitting a tree. We all know that sound. This was a dull thud."

As early in the season as it was, the grass around the tree in question had not yet been trimmed, so Buettell went over to help the golfer find his ball. What they also found was the reason for the unusual sound – the golf ball had beaned a newborn fawn that had been hidden in the grass by its mother.

And killed it dead.

"Popped Bambi right on the noggin," Buettell said. "That was a one-in-a-million shot, for sure."

Like a hole-in-one, said Buettell's wife, Melissa.

Except, of course, the poor sap with the club in his hand didn't have to buy drinks for the clubhouse. And he likely didn't get the burst of adrenaline that comes from a truly great shot.

"He probably felt bad about that the rest of his round," Buettell said. "I didn't run into him to ask him how (the rest of) his round went."

Anyone who has played golf in northern Wisconsin knows that deer can be, er, natural hazards. I've teed off from the white tees on Madeline Island GC over deer that refused to move from the red tees right in front to let me play through. A line drive would have been good for a venison feast.

Buettell said fawns are common, too, though they lose their charm in a very short time when they go from shaky-legged cute to green-piercing frisky. Still, he'd never seen the likes of this before.

"I've worked on golf courses all over the state for many years," he said, referring to the part-time labor that supplements his main business as "Muskie Matt," fishing guide. "I have never seen one like that. I have never seen one get whacked in the noggin like that."

The logical next step was to remove the carcass from the course, which usually means to a landfill, but Buettell had a different idea.

He asked if he could have the carcass so he could take it to a taxidermist and have it preserved. Stuffed fawns are popular with some in the North; you'll find them in wildlife museums and in taverns, which are sometimes one and the same. But most of those are either found as roadkill or had to be taken from their mother stillborn after she was killed. Some of those can challenge a taxidermist the way Tony Soprano's enemies challenge the undertaker.

But this fawn, the victim of such a clean hit, a one-in-a-million head shot that left no damage – aside from death, of course – was another matter. The taxidermist, Buettell said, "said it was one of the best ones he ever worked on."

It won't surprise you to know there are government regulations that cover such matters. Buettell knew he could do nothing with the carcass until the Department of Natural Resources checked the deer and tagged it, and because the DNR has lots to do, that couldn't happen overnight. So he put the fawn on ice for a few months – literally.

"It was in my freezer," said Melissa. "My kids were a little freaked when they reached in for ice cream."

But approval was finally obtained ("It died how?" the game warden asked.)

and Buettell took the fawn to Lax Taxidermy in Conover, where it was skinned, stuffed and mounted in a glass display case with native fauna around it. In the end Buettell was out maybe $1,200 but when he and Melissa presented the case to the Eagle River Area Chamber of Commerce and Visitors Center he felt it was all worth it.

"Well, A," he said, "I thought it was a good way to preserve a fawn. We get a lot of tourists around here ... "

As for B, he said, "That and throw a plaque in there with my guide service name on it."

That would be, if you are in the market for a fishing caddie, "Muskie Matt" at Casting Concepts Guide Service. If you cast with a slice, he's the man for you.

*****

After writing this column I heard from Mike Hilborn, a summer resident of the Eagle River area and the aforementioned golfer who launched the fateful, and fatal, shot.

"I'm not a sap and yes, I felt terrible, not only for the rest of the round but to this day," he said in an e-mail.

"I am an animal lover and for me this was like killing Bambi. What was truly shocking to me was that I was viewed as a hero by the locals here."

And, golfer that he is, Hilborn wanted to note one other thing:

"P.S. The shot was really a pretty good one, just slightly to the right. It just landed in the wrong place."

Bambi, were it possible, would agree.

Business booms for
Sid the Golf Ball Man

August 1995

We don't normally offer people the Witness Protection Program in *Wisconsin Golfer* but we've been asked – actually, ordered – to make an exception for Sid the Golf Ball Man.

"Don't go using my name," he growled. "You'll get me in hot soup. The state and federal will come around."

Well, I'm not above a little aiding and abetting an old man's anonymity if it will keep him out of the governmental rough. So no last names, no dollar amounts. And you would have to torture me with sharp, burning sticks to get me to reveal where I found him.

Oh, all right. Somewhere in Waukesha County, at the edge of a golf course.

He moved there 20 years ago, not intending to get into the golf ball business but open to opportunity if it should bounce his way.

"I got a couple of disks out of my back," he said, "and I'd go for a walk and see the golf balls and I'd pick 'em up.

Just "for the hell of it," he said, he put them in his yard in a bucket. "And the golfers started buying them."

Ray Kroc started small, too, and you know what happened there. One ball led to another – and luckily for Sid the boom in golf made lost balls a growth industry – and before you could say "Fore!" he had a shed out back with thousands of veteran balls, cleaned and sorted, to sell to the thousands of needy golfers who passed his backyard each summer. He put a big sign in

sight of the tee, hung a hammock between the garage and a tree and let the world come to him.

"GOLF BALLS FOR LESS," his shed now boasts in great big letters. "OVER 80,000 SOLD."

Really? I asked.

"Ah, that's bull----," he said at first, still thinking I might be a revenuer. But he hinted several times later that of all the misdemeanors he might be accused of, false advertising wasn't among them.

Not much of his stock comes from the course out back. Kids bring him big supplies of balls hawked from other courses, though there's a lot more competition on that end than there used to be. "It used to be, 10 years ago, golf courses would let people pick them up free of charge," he said. "Now they charge for every ball."

So what's up with golf balls these days? Titleist is most popular, followed by Top Flite and then probably Ultra, though in a world where lots of people hit golf balls off piers and boats and rooftops, every ball has a buyer.

"There is no such thing as a golf ball that is no good," he said. "You could have a ball that's got half its cover gone, they sell. I call 'em one-way balls, but they still sell at a pretty good price.

"Them colored ones first came out, they did pretty good. Now they're fading away. They went back to the white. The ladies like pink balls.

"The best ball, I say, is this one here, the Precept. I think China makes them. It works good all the way around, for everything. The Accutech – very, very good ball. Golf balls come in different sizes, too. Some of them are smaller – they're illegal, but some of them are smaller – and some are a little oversize. It used to be golfers didn't like logos, but now they do.

"They got floaters, too. Now, that don't make sense either. You hit a floater into the water and it floats, but how in the hell are you going to go out and get it?"

Even a business run from a hammock is not without its headaches, which can be caused by either golfers or their balls. He raised his cap to scratch an invisible wound he remembered well.

"I was sitting on the bench one day," he said, "and got hit right here. It took the skin and hair off right to the bone. I never saw so many stars in my life. If it had come in any lower it would have killed me."

And it's a thankless job, too. Everybody wants a deal, they accuse him of waxing the balls, they want a baker's dozen instead of 12 and some lose count when they pick out their own – but only in their favor.

"Now, there's only one person out of 20 who can put up with golfers' bull----. Some people will sell their soul for one golf ball," he said, but then he cackled. "I just happen to thrive on that stuff. I got about 10 answers for every one of their (lines). They're not kidding me any. I know when they come here they're going to go golfing. Regardless of all the bull, I know they're going to need balls."

Too true. Sid had to go then, off to his house in a city, but I can't tell you where. I headed off, too, carrying a bag of Precepts. If they were so good, I was thinking, how did they ever get lost?

St. Vince's real
passion was golf

January 2000

To paraphrase the sainted coach, winning isn't everything. Golf is.

Vincent Lombardi never said that, of course, but it was close to the truth. Golf, as it turns out, was one of Lombardi's passions. Winning at football was his Holy Grail but the golf course was his escape from perfection's demands.

Lombardi's love of golf – alas, often at the expense of his family obligations – was one of the many fascinating disclosures in "When Pride Still Mattered," the recent biography of Green Bay's iconic coach by Madison native David Maraniss, now a Pulitzer Prize-winning writer for the *Washington Post*.

Lombardi settled on golf as an escape as early as his stint at West Point, where he was an assistant coach in the 1950s. But the ultimate competitor couldn't merely relax; he had to make a game of golf, and not just for him. The school had an odd, 10-hole course and it was Lombardi's habit to pay his caddie $1 a hole, but only if no balls were lost.

It was up to the caddie to find his ball, in woods or water, or the cost would be deducted from his pay. It was just Lombardi's nature, Maraniss wrote, to test the youngster who toted his bag.

Golf as refuge was never so important as in 1963, and not just for the Packers' coach. Early that year, after a long investigation into gambling by professional football players, NFL Commissioner Pete Rozelle announced that Paul Hornung – legendary "Golden Boy" and perhaps Lombardi's favorite

player – was being suspended for his involvement.

After the sentence was handed down, Hornung was found by reporters at a golf course, where he escaped to the clubhouse to prepare a statement. And, warned by Rozelle that an announcement was imminent, Maraniss wrote, "Lombardi, like Hornung, had fled to the sanctuary of a golf course."

Where else?

"If there was anything in Lombardi's life that approached his obsession with football during his time in Green Bay, it was golf. He attended Mass every morning out of a combination of habit and spiritual need, but he would have played 365 days a year if it had been possible, wholly out of love," Maraniss wrote.

Of course, when the tundra was frozen the greens were, too. But Lombardi – a member at Oneida G&CC – once played two days after Christmas, clad in long underwear and an ear-flapped cap.

Earplugs were necessary for some around him. Lombardi's famous temper was usually the fifth man in his foursome. "You could hear him anywhere on the course when he missed a shot," one of his partners said. "It was very R-rated and guttural ... "

He possessed neither an athlete's body nor a golfer's textbook swing. It was stiff and jerky, and no less an authority than Max McGee said, "He looked ugly out there. You'd play a round with him and think he'd shot 110."

But Lombardi, who actually played to about a 13 handicap, was ever the gamer. In bestball events he was said to be able to will himself to better shots when his partner had put their chances in peril. Of course, as one partner noted, his very presence was worth a few shots on the first tee.

"The other team would be three or four down before they got over the fact that they were playing against Vince Lombardi."

But Lombardi wanted much more than to simply intimidate his opponents. He once told a friend that "the toughest single battle he had in life was his golf game." The man thought Lombardi was kidding, but he was dead serious.

"I'm going to tell you why. Because I have the toughest opponent in my golf game. ME. I'm trying to improve my score, and it's just me. I'm always fighting to get better against myself. That is tough."

It might seem odd that a biography of a football coach – though "When Pride Still Mattered" is much more than a sports book – should say something so interesting about golf, but there you have it. In the end, this man who was a giant on so many levels was just like us, as entranced by the great game of golf as bedeviled by it.

Something in common with St. Vince. Who knew?

The kingdom
of Michael Murphy

December 1998

I had been to a fair number of book events but this was a new one to me. Michael Murphy had been to many more over the last 25 years but the menu at his recent Milwaukee reading was a first for him, as well.

"I never," Murphy said, though not complaining, "had this much whiskey before a talk."

To local members of the Shivas Irons Society, they who had ordained that guests and speaker should have "a wee dram of Scotch" in Murphy's honor, it was high praise indeed. And while not officially among their number, I couldn't complain. Maybe a wee dram is what it takes to bring Murphy's mystical take on the grandest game into clearer understanding. It couldn't hurt.

Murphy is something of a cult figure in golf circles, though he declines to use the term cult in discussing his fans. In 1972 he wrote "Golf in the Kingdom," a novel that explored the deepest secrets of golf as revealed in the teachings of the mysterious but amazingly talented Scottish professional, Shivas Irons. Playing a round of golf with Irons at the Burningbush GC, Murphy becomes involved in the pursuit of "true gravity," a sort of mental bliss that grows out of the game's spiritual energy.

Some might think that more than a wee dram of mumbo-jumbo but Murphy found an audience. The book, he said, "has legs of its own." It has sold more than 100,000 copies annually in recent years and been translated into seven languages. Devoted fans formed the Shivas Irons Society to explore

golf's mystical nature in greater detail, and Clint Eastwood is working on a film adaptation.

No less than the novelist John Updike called it "a golf classic if any exists in our day." The noted philosopher Payne Stewart once said he didn't understand a word of the book's second part – an examination of the mystery of the hole, the pleasures of practice and "occult backlash" – but then Payne Stewart wouldn't understand In and Out on a swinging door without a hint. And while Bill Murray's "be the ball" schtick in "Caddyshack" had fun with Murphy's inner game, Murray has confessed to being a "Golf in the Kingdom" fan.

Murphy was in Milwaukee as part of a book tour for the sequel, "The Kingdom of Shivas Irons," written in large part because of the huge number of otherworldly experiences golfers have shared with Murphy since his first book was published. There was the man who told of a moment of true clarity when he saw a ball marker the size of a dime from the tee, or the woman who found the light of the setting sun was replaced by another light.

"I feel at times like Father Murphy taking confessions from golfers," he said in an interview. "They tell me the most amazing experiences.

"Most people do not have these sorts of dramatic experiences. But all of these experiences, as far out as they seem, happened to people. The core experiences are true. The question is, how much is out there?"

Mystic golf is not his main work. The founder of Esalen Institute in Big Sur, Calif., Murphy's principle interest is the human potential movement, but the pursuit of world philosophies is in many ways like the pursuit of the perfect swing. His own game now is limited to half a dozen rounds a year, often in the company of Shivas Irons chapters.

He's amused by the following, and flattered. I asked him, though, if he sometimes wanted to scream out, like Captain Kirk at a Trekkies convention, "Get a life!"

"No," he laughed, "it hasn't gotten that far. So far I've gotten a kick out of the whole thing. The events I've been to have been a lot of fun. It's a rich mixture of golf and philosophy sessions. I hate the thought it would turn into a cult, or something embarrassing. In Zen it's called the 'stink of Zen,' when you just talk it to death. So it's like everything in life. You need a balance."

But many who attended Murphy's talk were clearly in his camp. They discussed golf's many layers, nodded in understanding when Murphy mentioned how many golf professionals used golf psychologists or practiced meditation as often as putting and – hey, you want mystical? – agreed the rainbow over Davis Love's head when he won the PGA Championship in 1997 was truly a sign from above. It was evidence, as Murphy said, "there was actual work being done on the other side."

Food for thought, isn't it? And I don't mean the Scotch.

Golf balls and golf memories

November 2000

The other day while in Door County on business – no, really – I took time to try a new course, The Orchards at Egg Harbor. After a sparkling front side deteriorated into my usual woods-and-water game, I left with haunted thoughts of what might have been, and with a golf ball for the basement wall.

Another ball, I should say.

Just a few days earlier someone had asked if I collect anything and I paused before answering, a bit sheepishly, golf balls. It's a step up from the match books I collected as a boy in the 1950s, but it's well short of collecting something valuable like Mark Twain first editions or Andy Warhol soup cans. It is cheaper than collecting ex-wives, like Donald Trump, I suppose.

My practical friend Earl can't understand spending good money on golf balls that will never know a tee. He only collects balls he finds on his daily walks past Maple Bluff CC (the rich, it seems, don't chase their mistakes). And frankly, there are days when I'm stepping up to pay for a new box of ammunition that I think of the balls on my basement wall and wonder myself if it makes any sense. There are nearly 100 now, mounted on wooden racks my father-in-law made in his workshop, every one as unsmacked as the day it was bought.

The guy who came up with the idea of selling balls that won't be played will go into the marketing hall of fame with the genius who added "repeat" to the directions on shampoo bottles and suddenly sold twice as much product. The golf ball is already the classic example of planned obsolesence, as anyone who ever dunked a new sleeve on a water hole can attest. And it's not like I take them down and play with them, after all.

The best I can say is I notice them once in a while, and that's enough.

I collect according to one strict rule – only logo balls from courses I have personally played go on the wall, unless I feel like breaking the rule. That explains the Richard Nixon Library and Birthplace ball and the Grateful Dead ball, both representing strange trips this country has known. It also explains the Packers ball, the Badgers ball, the red and white Merry Christmas ball and the cheddar-yellow cheese ball.

But the rest conform to the rule, and in the process serve as a reverse road map of my golfing life.

There are balls from Riverside and Blackhawk golf courses in Janesville, where I learned to play, and from Pleasant View in Middleton where we played in high school. Of course, the ball doesn't say Pleasant View; it features a red running ram and reads Goat Hill, which is what everyone calls it anyway. I like a golf ball with a sense of humor.

On one shelf are balls from California and New England, from Georgia and South Carolina, all stamps on my golfing visa. On another is a golf ball from Augusta National, which I didn't play, of course, but where I attended the Masters this year for Sunday's final round. Close enough.

I can't look at the ball from the Grand Hotel course on Mackinac Island without thinking of the horse-drawn cart that carried us from the ninth green to the 10th tee. If you don't think a golf cart can be romantic, think again.

Like history? There's a Tuscumbia CC Centennial Ball from 1998, and that's a profile of the father of our country on the Washington County GC ball. Birds? Rock River Hills GC in Horicon and Idlewild GC in Sturgeon Bay feature flying geese, Krueger in Beloit offers a hummingbird and Princeton Valley in Eau Claire offers a goofy feathered flyer called Birdie. Travel? The ball from Adare GC was imported from County Killarney. I can taste the smooth, black pleasure that is Guinness when I see it.

And that's the point, isn't it? Long after the back nine failures have been lost in time, the latest addition to my wall will tell of a fabulous fall afternoon in the hills of Egg Harbor, where I took a three-hour walk that even my game couldn't have spoiled. On snowy winter days I'll notice that ball and feel the sun again.

Collect golf balls? On second thought, not me. I collect memories.

At long last – Augusta

May 2000

I'm the last guy you'd ever think of as a name dropper but there I was on Masters Sunday, standing with my friends just off the ninth green at Augusta National GC – Bobby Jones' own course, you know, haunted by the ghosts of Hogan and Sarazen and so many more – when a woman and her son arrived looking for a view.

Of course we let them through to stand in front of us. They were shorter than we were.

No, I'm kidding. We let them through because they were Ardena and Qass Singh, wife and son of the golfer Vijay Singh, of the Fiji Singhs, who at that moment was leading the tournament and about to hit his approach shot on the par-4 ninth. I looked at my friends and they looked at me. The Masters, as CBS relentlessly tells us, is an event like no other. And there we were, not only on hand and in person but right in the thick of it.

They say the Masters doesn't really start until the back nine on Sunday but Singh jump-started his finishing stretch by hitting that shot to within 18 inches. Applause all around. Augusta's famous greens are faster than a hungry pickpocket, but Singh was below the hole and looking at as much of a gimme as you'll find on that golf course.

Still, just for good measure my friend Tom crossed his fingers and whispered to Qass that he might do the same. The young Mr. Singh, who we learned later had already slipped a good luck note in his poppa's bag, agreed.

He crossed the first two fingers on his right hand, then the other two, then did the same with his left hand and in case that wasn't enough he crossed his thumbs, too. The putt dropped, hand slaps were exchanged, his dad went on to win the tournament and took home a loud but coveted sports coat and a check for $828,000.

We took home some hats and shirts and memories. Anyone who argued Singh had the better day would get an argument from us.

A few years ago I was privileged to attend the first Rose Bowl the Wisconsin Badgers played in since Bucky's grandpa was a gleam in his great grandpa's eye. Like many Wisconsin fans, I announced at the game's conclusion that now I could die a happy man, preferably before the credit card bill arrived. It wasn't that I lacked other dreams; I did, but breaking 80 and getting to see the Masters in person were up there with finding the Hope Diamond in my wife's jewelry box, preferably before she did.

Now all that's left is death and shooting a 79, one implausible, the other inevitable. Those of you who have seen me play might prepare your condolences now.

Masters badges and state secrets are equal players in the intrigue game. I'm not at liberty to divulge exactly how we were able to obtain entry to Augusta National except to say that my brother has moved into first place in my will, should anything be left after I: a) die, or b) snake in a 3-footer for 79 and buy drinks until bar time. Suffice to say, on the likely chance that there would be a few extra badges for Sunday's round if members of a certain corporate group went home early, I rounded up two friends of some 35 years and headed for Augusta. There were, and there we were.

In my other life I've walked on battleships and traveled far and wide; I've covered actual presidents and interviewed wannabes. But watching Jack Nicklaus play Amen Corner on Masters Sunday is an event like, well, no other. Never mind he was among the first out on Sunday after a rough Saturday showing, the first time in his life he failed to break 80 at Augusta. (Jack and I have very different problems.) What true golf fan wouldn't want to see that?

We did it all, or as much as we could given the crowds. We marveled at the beauty of the dogwoods and azaleas, gawked at the players we never see in Milwaukee, stood in line to buy souvenirs (as much to help us remember as to make our other friends jealous) and reveled in the golf. Amazingly, we found seats in the bleachers at fabled 15 in time to watch the leaders go through. My friend Tim had a guarantee of free drinks for a year if he could get his hat – which bore the logo of a Milwaukee bar – on TV. In what can only be called good news for the bar owner's chance of making it, that didn't happen.

But that was about the only disappointment, even if we only heard the final putt drop because there was no way to see it. On the way out we even saw Tiger Woods, having just missed another opportunity to begin to cement the status some prematurely awarded him after his first Masters win, attempt to drive off in his courtesy car, only to get stuck in traffic. Wait a few minutes, then wait 'til next year.

Our wait, though, was over. It was a great day. Though it would have been nice if the press had given my friend Tom credit for his role in the victory.

Author's Note: I have not found the Hope Diamond, and I still have not broken 80.

The caddie's got a gun

September 2006

Emerson Farrell has a photograph, maybe 6 inches by 12, that he takes great delight in scrutinizing. In it are the faces of more than 40 boys and young men, many scruffy, if you'll permit the judgment, about half of them in flat caps, a few smoking cigarettes, some hidden from the viewer by the heads of others in front. A few are smiling, most are dead serious. At 93, and more than 70 years since the photo was taken, Farrell can't remember most of the names now, just some of the nicknames and even then not where they came from.

But the faces prompt stories, if not names.

History and golf go together like a ball and tee. We all know of St. Andrews and the Toms Morris, old and young. Get Ben Crenshaw going and he'll tell stories of Harvey Penick and Ben Hogan and all the old greats. Get Jack Nicklaus going and he'll tell stories of, well, Jack Nicklaus. I got Emerson Farrell going and the history that flowed was of a little Northwoods golf course where the swells of Hollywood and Chicago and other distant places came to play golf, and those boys and men in flat caps lugged their clubs for pocket change.

"I'll be honest with you," he said of the photograph. "There's about three left out of the group. They're all gone now."

That's why his stories are important, enough a part of the local story in Eagle River they were submitted for a book to be published in 2007 for the city's sesquicentennial. The faces in Farrell's photograph were of caddies at Eagle Waters GC in Eagle River (now Lake Forest Resort and Club), where Farrell looped from the 1920s and into the 1930s, back when area resorts and taverns were wide open, offering slot machines and table games and other good times to all comers. If some of those characters came by their wealth in questionable ways, well, when the Depression raged there was no percentage in being too choosy.

"In those days," Farrell said, "you couldn't be too fussy. You had to go where you could make a buck. A single bag was 50 cents for nine holes, a dollar for 18. A double was just twice that, and believe me, a double was a load. Some of those guys had the heaviest bags."

Of course, that was only summer work. At the end of the season it was off to the lumber camps or other winter jobs.

The club was a nine-holer, built to serve what was called the Everett Colony that included summer cottages at Catfish and Cranberry Lakes. The resorts in the Eagle River area catered to all sorts of summer visitors but especially to the famous, the infamous and those with "money to burn," as Farrell put it.

"Now that golf course had more famous people," he said. "They came from all over the world. The parking lot had the most beautiful cars in the world, Cadillacs, Lincolns ... it was the poorest people in the world (working for) the richest people in the world.

"I caddied for this movie star. I said, 'Where's all that jewelry you used to wear?' She said, 'There's a depression on.'"

Farrell laughed. Eagle River was in depression, too, but it wasn't much different from the good times.

Eagle River Historical Society records say that Walter Hagen played there, as did the actresses Joan Crawford and Janet Gaynor. Elizabeth Taylor, who spent a fair bit of time in northern Wisconsin as a girl, was there as well, and Chicago Mayor Ed Kelly, who had a place on one of the lakes, was a regular.

"I caddied for Mayor Kelly," Farrell said. "He played all the time. When we were on the course his bodyguard would always say, 'Here, kid, you carry this. It's too heavy when I play.'"

"This" was the bodyguard's gun, which Farrell would tote along with the clubs. "When I had the bodyguard's gun I had to be right with them all the time. So I was Mayor Kelly's bodyguard when he was on the course."

And his entertainment as well. Farrell said they often put a ball on the tee and told him to shoot it off with the gun, which he always did. "Nowadays," he said, still savoring the moment, "you'd probably get arrested for some of the things we used to do."

Caddies did well when the course was humming. "Us caddies could make almost as much as a carpenter," Farrell said. Of course, he added for perspective, "I had to walk five miles to the course to caddie, then walk home five miles. But then we bought a Model T Ford for $15, oh boy, that was a big thing! In one part of the parking lot would be $15 cars and in another, $3,000 cars. (But) they were easy people to get along with. No problems."

Farrell never got seriously into golf. He worked lots of jobs through his lifetime, lived in California and Illinois, but otherwise stayed true to Eagle River, where he now lives next to his old family farm. When we talked, though, he still sounded intrigued by the offer Kelly's bodyguard, a Capt. Berry, made.

"He always said to me in the fall, 'Kid, come with me to Chicago. I'll have you on a beat in six months.' 'Well, no,' I said, 'I'm just a green country kid. I don't think I'd do very well in Chicago.' I didn't understand city ways, you know?"

Laughing again, he said, "You know, I should have gone."

The bet

August 1993

The bet was the thing.

It wasn't supposed to be, of course; when the Holy Name Seminary High School Class of 1968 got together in Madison again this summer, it wasn't even on the schedule.

Dinner, a little dancing, some reminiscing – maybe a nap, at our age – those were on the schedule.

Indeed, memories should have ruled the day for our group, the class that had (by and large) survived the tumultuous quarter-century that brought us Vietnam, Watergate, political assassinations, John, Paul, George, Ringo and Timothy Leary, bell-bottom pants, and all the other successes and excesses of our generation.

So what did some of us spend all Friday night and a bleary part of Saturday morning discussing?

Golf, of course. Precisely: How many strokes our foursome had to give the other foursome at the nine-hole outing Saturday afternoon.

Amazing. Ours was a small class, not everyone could make the reunion and not everyone who did played golf. So it shouldn't have been that difficult to set up a couple of foursomes, step to the tee and hit the damn ball.

But when Chuck the English teacher drew up the teams, set the handicaps and offered the enemy 14 strokes to make it even (as his teammate, I thought that most generous) you would have thought he'd asked them to play blind and putt with a bent mashie, for all they howled.

There was discussion, then debate, then argument. Then yelling, but only when necessary to make a sensible point above the other guy's selfish jabbering, which was most of the time.

You know those peace talks at the United Nations where everybody is speaking a different language and interpreters are chattering and it gets so loud and confusing you can't tell what's going on? Like that.

"Fourteen strokes!" Tim the leasing agent kept screaming.

"Fourteen!!!" Why don't I just hand you my wallet now?"

He was so loud he didn't hear Chuck say that would be OK with him.

Tim wanted 28. Chuck said that was ridiculous, and I might have mentioned myself that was as stupid as pantyhose on a boar pig.

Tim protested like a politician charged with graft and said the match was off. Then it was back on, but Tim's side wanted at least 20 because Fred was so busy being a Navy commander he hadn't been playing and somebody else's game was off and blah, blah, blah.

At one point, it got so complicated that there was a side bet on whether the 14 strokes would turn out to be within 20 of the actual scores, or something like that. It got confusing.

Tim the police officer tried to help out, but he doesn't know a press from a push, so that went nowhere. The rest just offered help once in a while: Jim the fish fry king; Tom the psychiatrist, who in his long, white beard resembles an Amish rabbi gone golfing; and Tim the paper company magnate who plays weekly but hadn't broken 62 for nine holes this year.

When my wife said, "Why don't you just play for fun?" we all looked at her, for once men of the '90s able to say out loud – "Women, they just don't get it."

So it went, through dinner and dessert, through the evening back at the hotel, into the early morning. When we went to bed – about 0200 hours, if I remember Commander Fred's watch correctly, which I'm not sure I do – the bet was unresolved.

A very few hours later, I ran into Tim the leasing agent in the lobby.

"Just how much," he asked in a froggy, morning-after voice, "are we playing for?"

A buck, I said.

He gave me a look you'd expect from a man who'd spent $60 or $70 on food and drink while arguing about a $1 bet. Let's play, he said.

So we teed it up at Pleasant View GC in Middleton, where we had played in high school. It turned out peacetime had been good to Fred's game. He matched Tim the leasing agent's 44. Tim the paper magnate recorded the first par of his life on the second hole and the second on the third, if you follow me there. Chuck was low man with a 30-something, which says a lot about teacher vacations. I won't bore you with my problems except to say the Packers should score so many 6s.

Oh, the bet. That's funny. Between sitting over a few cold beers, telling a few final lies and heading back to get ready for the reunion, nobody actually collected on that.

We also never got around to Watergate or the Beatles. But it was sure fun arguing with those guys again.

This will go down as the summer of sandbagging, but it didn't all take place in flood-ravaged Prairie du Chien.

Walter Hagen, I'd know you anywhere

November 2001

What's in a name? Ask the Little Leaguer named Stan "The Kid" Musial, the new brush salesman named Fuller or the blind date your friend set you up with – name of Madonna.

Expectations, my friends. Names raise them.

The subject arises because I was recently seated at a luncheon next to a man who introduced himself as Walter Hagen.

"Wow," I said. "How's the swing?" But this Walter Hagen wasn't THAT Walter Hagen. In fact, he played golf but once in his life and his name, his wife said, was part of the reason. Who wants to go to the first tee lugging a legend's name and a who's-that swing?

It started me thinking, so I called a few other Wisconsin folks to see what it's like to carry the names of famous golfers.

"Or," said John Daly of Madison, "maybe they carry our names."

Whatever. For the most part, it turns out, there is little pressure in sharing the name of one of our sport's gods, assuming you are secure in your own 18 handicap and capable of taking the teasing that comes when you hook and slice like a human.

"He gets teased all the time," said Jerri Watson of Madison, speaking of her husband Tom.

But occasionally there are perks to offset the abuse. A few years ago, she said, they went to Gene Autry's golf resort in Palm Springs and, as you would expect, made a reservation under the name Tom Watson.

"We got a great suite that day," Jerri said. "They put us in one of the great suites."

Any confusion over her husband's identity ended, she said, "after they saw him." But if it was mistaken identity that got them that suite, it was fun while it lasted.

David Duval of Two Rivers said his name is a matter of curiosity for tele-marketers, but that's about it. David Duval of Hudson, who does play golf a few times a year, says the name is no problem on the course, but it's a bit of a hurdle getting there.

"It is fun when I try and make a tee time," he said. "They'll say, 'What's your name?' I say, 'David Duval.' They say, 'Right.'"

Half the time he has to produce his ID just to show he really is who he thinks he is, he said, but once he got a free round for the trouble.

Tom Lehman of Eau Claire, who was a golf course manager in his earlier years, also had to produce ID once – to show to Tom Lehman.

It was at a tournament in Las Vegas when the two Toms met. "My sister was along and she said, 'Tom Lehman, meet Tom Lehman.' I pulled out my license and showed him and he said, 'You're one hell of a golfer,'" said our Tom Lehman. "ESPN wanted to interview him but he held that back until he talked to me and had his picture taken with me. He was real nice to me."

By coincidence, our Tom had just finished watching the other Tom in the Las Vegas tourney when I called. Like other Wisconsin namesakes of PGA Tour players, he has a special rooting interest.

Or, as Jerry Kelly of Appleton better put it, "I wish I had his money."

John Daly of Milwaukee said the name can be fun during church golf out-ings, though the novelty of being tied to such a meteoric personality wore off some time ago. Three rehabs and four wives will do that, apparently.

But Madison's John Daly, who loves the game despite the pain it causes him, takes the association in stride and if a bit of secondary celebrity is visited upon him, well, that's gravy. Two years ago, when he bought a new set of irons, the clerk in the golf shop considered giving him a discount if he could post the check on the wall.

"The guy who sold them to me was half serious, because he called the man-ager to see if he could do it," he said. It would have been truth in advertising, sort of, but it didn't happen.

Then there was the day at the Greater Milwaukee Open when Daly, after leaving a corporate tent, inadvertantly left his nametag on when he returned to the course. At one hole, he heard a fan say to his friend that this was where John Daly had almost driven the green, do you remember? The friend, who had noticed our Daly's nametag over the other guy's shoulder, remarked slyly that John Daly was right behind him. No, the friend said, you're crazy.

Want to bet? the other guy said. And of course his friend did, $5, whereupon he turned around and saw ... John Daly.

"I just pointed to my nametag. He said 'No way, show me your driver's license' ... he swore, went right up to his buddy and paid him the five bucks. Unfortunately, I didn't make any money on it."

But then there was the day at Lake Arrowhead this summer when he hit a typically errant shot and the search was on. A man in his group found a ball stamped "John Daly" and threw it to him, and while it was not even close to the one he had hit into the woods how could he deny it was his ball if his name was on it?

"I keep it right it my car," he said. "It's a signature John Daly. I didn't take an extra stroke on it, either. It was definitely my ball."

I couldn't reach a Nancy Lopez who was listed in Waukesha County, any of four Peter Jacobsens around the state, a Steve Stricker from central Wisconsin or even one of seven of our state's Bobby Joneses to discuss the matter. And one Sergio Garcia of Milwaukee wasn't home when I called. The woman who answered, however, assured me that he wasn't the one on TV.

"I wish it was," she said. "But it's not him."

It's not just a name. It's a burden.

Hit the number,
or die trying

May 2006

A rnold Palmer said a golfer must have mixed feelings about shooting his or her age. It's exciting, yes, but you have to be pretty well up there in years for it to happen.

I wouldn't know about that – not yet. I played golf yesterday and only came within 37 shots of my age, but while I'm a lousy golfer, at least I've got time on my side. The question is, can I get 37 shots better before I get 37 years older?

The reality is, of course, that most of us will never come close to shooting our age, which is one of golf's most elusive goals. Any chump can get lucky and fall into a hole-in-one and, if properly handicapped on the right day, take a few bucks from a much better player. But those of us who can't dream of shooting in the 70s when we're only in our 50s shouldn't hope for an age score in this lifetime.

So no, I didn't sign up for the "Shoot Your Age Championship" that was network TV's latest idea for a so-called reality show, the chance to go head to head with Arnold Palmer and Gary Player and 80 other gray-haired competitors. Interesting concept, though. Everyone played from the same tees, par was each player's age and the minute your score surpassed your age you were out of the tournament. No naps between nines, either.

Still, it's not impossible. Wisconsin golfers Dave Uelman and Hal Knuth, who both winter in Florida, were intrigued by the idea of the "Shoot Your Age" tourney, and either one could have been a contender. In fact, on the day

I called to talk about shooting his age, Uelman, who plays out of North Shore CC, had just recorded a nice little 78, one shot less than the number of candles on his last cake.

Uelman first shot his age when he was 69, playing in a club event in Naples with a pro in his foursome as witness. He didn't think much about the possibility until it came right down to the end.

"I knew I had to par the last hole," he said. "I had about a 12-foot putt. I told the pro I had to make it to shoot my age. He said, 'Well, I'll give it to you.'"

Uelman didn't take the gimme. He made the putt, giving him the first of many age scores.

Manuel de la Torre, the estimable teaching pro at Milwaukee CC who is 84, also shot his age at 69, and every year since then. At 69 it wasn't a big goal, he said. "You only have that goal when you pass 80."

But, he said, the more you want it the harder it gets. "If you go out there with the intention of shooting your age, you probably aren't going to be able to do it. It's something that just happens."

As evidence, Hal Knuth.

"It just sort of happened," Knuth said of the first time. "I thought about it when there were three holes left and I thought, well, this could be the time. And I parred the last three holes."

That was when he was 71. He's 76 now and has shot his age in each succeeding year and expects he'll be able to do so for a few more years. But it's not getting any easier. This spring he shot a 75 and as the round advanced felt "so damn nervous," mostly because at 76 he isn't playing as well as he was a few years ago. He's an 8 handicap now, where three years ago he was a 4.

"So you can see what's happening," he said. "Some say the older you get the more chances you get. I'm not a believer in that." There might not be much difference between the ages of 70 and 75, he said, "but once they become older it's tougher. You can't concentrate as well and you don't hit the ball as far."

Ah, length. Uelman said any golfer entertaining the notion of shooting his or her age must be competitive, willing to practice and eager to play tournament golf to get better. "You've got to have a short game, because at this age you're not going to be hitting the greens ... you have to be able to chip and putt."

"And," he said, "you have to buy a lot of equipment."

Technology is an aging player's best friend.

But not even rocket science can help every player. "You don't come to it late in life," as Uelman put it. You have to be good and you have to stay good. Knuth once played in a "super seniors" event with a man who was 87, and who turned in a tidy 78. "It was really something to see," he said. "I was wide-eyed all the way around the course."

Impressive, yes, but not a record. According to a Web site that listed age-shooter records, a Canadian golfer named Arthur Thompson shot his age in 1972 when he was 103. The youngest golfer to shoot his age, by the way, was Bob Hamilton, a pro who turned in a 59 at age 59. And one Frank Bailey of Abilene, Texas, was said to have accomplished the feat every year between the age of 71 and 98, a total of 2,623 times.

All in all, cause for hope. On a bad day I can shoot 103.

Now, as they say, I should live so long.

Waushara CC still shows scars from tornado of '92

July 1994

I t's easy to joke about a wind strong enough to straighten the bend in a dogleg, unless you've seen one.

The storm that ripped through Waushara County two years ago in August was one of those. It was a massive tornado that touched down south of Wautoma, then roared across the ground for miles of destruction.

No one would say, then or now, the damage to Waushara CC was the most significant in town. A woman died, after all, dozens were injured and dozens more were left homeless. In its twisted wake the tornado left millions of dollars of damage that even now has not been completely repaired, replaced or removed. But the course was damaged heavily when the tornado played through that night, and, in many ways, was changed forever.

The hickory trees that made No. 14 a dogleg, for example? Gone with the wind. Now you can shoot straight across.

"It really made a lot of difference on a few holes," said club manager George Ray. "It dramatically changed them. It's a completely different golf course, really, because all the strategically placed trees blew over."

That's not all. Club members have a new, spacious and modern clubhouse now, but they got it for the same reason they pull a new ball from its sleeve. They lost their old one.

"There's millions of people who never experience a tornado," Ray said. "So they don't realize what it's like."

It's shocking, at first. Ray suffered not so much as a lost branch where he lives nearby. So when he went to the club the next morning he wasn't sure what to expect.

It was still dark so he carried a flashlight. But there was something eerie; as he climbed the hill he felt out of place and disoriented. He realized all the trees he knew as landmarks were gone.

"I called the boss and told him we're going to have to have a new club-house," Ray said. "He didn't think too much of that early in the morning."

Insurance paid for part of that cost, though the new house was larger and that added $100,000 to the tab. But there was no insurance for much of the loss, especially the trees which were older than the course itself.

"How do you put a price on a 100-year-old tree?" Ray asked.

In all, maybe a thousand trees were destroyed by the storm, most large ones. The tornado was rising as it passed through so it skipped over small, young trees and sheared the tops off anything of size, leaving tall and painfully ugly stumps.

"We left some of those as reminders," Ray said.

Anywhere a tornado plays hell, the calm after the storm is followed by days of whining chain saws. Volunteers by the hundreds flocked to Waushara County in the following weeks to clear trees, put roofs on open houses, repair windows and begin to restore the trappings of everyday life. Golf was part of that.

"We had umpteen people working on the golf course for two weeks," Ray said. Some were club members, some were from other golf clubs who came to help fellow golfers in their time of need and some were local residents who also play the course. Others were Mennonite volunteers, a community of good-hearted folk who wouldn't know a wedge from a bowling pin but didn't care. The Red Cross and Salvation Army brought meals each day, and while in some respects the recovery continues today, the worst damage was put right.

"Two weeks after the tornado we were playing the back nine," Ray said, "and a week later the front nine."

But the storm was not without its final insults. When it damaged a mainte-nance building and ripped the sides off cart sheds, it was fickle in its destruc-tion.

"The tornado picked (my cart) up and turned it around and set it outside," Ray said. "I really do believe mine was the most damaged in the whole stupid thing."

Except for the last of the cleanup and the sheared off reminders on so many holes, that's all in the past now. The course, begun in the 1920s and expanded to 18 holes in the 1970s, is adding nine holes that should open this fall. And it has purchased additional land to build again when planned widening of Highway 21/73 gobbles up tees and greens on the lower end.

If you've lived through a storm that straightened doglegs, you can handle highway construction. It certainly puts a missed 2-footer for the match in perspective. A little, anyway.

A caddie grows up

June 1998

The other day I went with my wife to the one-stop, indoor-outdoor, two-level, lighted, air-controlled driving range, pro shop and all-around golf emporium, learning academy and kid golf summer camp – plus batting cages for that kid gone wrong.

Not satisfied with my help – "Hit it farther" apparently doesn't do it any-more – my wife wanted to kick off the season with a videotaped swing analysis. So while she made her small-screen debut in the arms of the head pro at one end of the downstairs, indoor, lighted, etc. range, I swatted a bucket of balls at the wall and thought about how far golf has come.

When I was a kid, back when Kennedy was president and graphite a gleam in some designer's eye, golf was so much simpler.

Not the game. Golf has always been more complicated than love itself. But the way we approached it was surely simpler. And it was always fun.

I started playing in grade school. My hometown, Janesville, had the respect-ed 18-hole Riverside GC, but I really started playing more when the city fathers (there were no city mothers back then) built the nine-hole Blackhawk GC a short bike ride from my house.

It was a pretty rugged test. It was thickly wooded and the pasture at the back end heavily thistled, so you needed lots of balls to play. Lots of evenings we would ride down and scour the rough for golf balls, then ride back by day to give them back one swing at a time. We didn't care; we loved it. Today I couldn't imagine riding a bike with a golf bag strapped across my back but it was how we got around then, and yes, I know I sound like some nostalgic geezer here.

Lessons? They were for school. Golf was for when school was out. And swing analysis? Please. Golf was what happened between the first tee and the ninth green, which may explain why my scores never improved much in the years I scuffed around Blackhawk, even after many of those troublesome trees had been cleared out.

Later I got to play Janesville CC on caddie days, though my looping days were as unspectacular as my golf game. The country club was on top of a hill and I was always distracted by the knowledge that bigger caddies were coasting home on my bike while I was lugging doubles for some husband and wife who hit in different directions.

But I kept playing, and kept playing mostly mediocre golf, and it wasn't until my late 30s that I took my first lesson.

There I was, a decade later, in the institute of higher links learning called Milwaukee Family Golf Center, where there were no excuses for not getting help and getting better.

The game is still complicated, but the approach to it is appropriately complex. The menu ranges from junior golf camps to a swing development program for new players and even a pro level program – a regimen of 46 private and group classes over 10 months designed to leave the student with the ability to play par golf.

I was tempted to sign up, if only to test the guarantee.

It only makes sense. Golf has exploded in popularity. Equipment has gotten better – and much more expensive – and it stands to reason that if you have more invested in the game you want more out of it.

Golf, if you let it or want it to, can go from mere pastime to lifestyle. The golf center can even be booked for your kid's birthday party (cake not included, additional charge if supervision must be provided).

I've changed. I want to get better, so I buy the clubs, take the lessons, take the game more seriously. I even drive a car to the course now. The trick is to do all that and still retain the thing that drew me in as a bike-riding boy – the fun that is a day of golf.

If play isn't fun, it's work. Then you ought to have your head examined, not your swing.

The Big Wait

January 1996

I was at my desk at the newspaper that employs me one chilly day, scanning stories coming in on the wire (hey, it makes you look busy) when a piece slugged "Golftips" popped onto the screen. It was about making the proper turn, how overturning is bad, how your shoulders should lead the way, 70 percent of your weight should shift to your right foot and your knee should be braced but still flexed.

Olga Korbut couldn't do all that at once, but never mind. I moved right along to a four-part series on getting in shape for skiing – and I don't even ski. Somehow, a philosophical treatise on the hippy-hippy swing seemed as out of place as frost on a putter, this being the Season of the Big Wait.

The Big Wait is not Craig Stadler's swing problem. It is that period when snow and cold turn golf into a made-for-TV thing, which is also when those sadists who run TV sports schedule tournaments in places like Hawaii and Jamaica so in addition to not being able to play the game we love, we snowbirds with clipped wings must stare bitterly at the privileged who can. Not funny, mon.

In Wisconsin, the Big Wait starts earlier for some than for others. There are the wimps, who view golf like white belts and shoes, not to be enjoyed after Labor Day or before Memorial Day. There are others who escape the courses when the geese chase them off and a small but hardy band of others – I admit membership to this bunch – who trudge on bravely until the geese have in turn been chased off by snowdrifts.

Last December at Kettle Hills GC near Milwaukee, my opponent made a cheap, cheesy par by bouncing a too-short wimpy shot off a frozen pond fronting the par-3 12th. I personally would have been embarrassed to take a 3 with such a shot but Eric had no such shame. Last winter I took up snowshoeing and one Sunday afternoon at Brown Deer Park I started thinking, "You know, if I had a 5-iron and an orange ball ... "

This year, tragically, my own Big Wait began early. I was out running one day in October – on clear pavement, in broad daylight – when I tripped on nothing and fell hard. Aside from bloodying both knees quite nicely, I rolled over on my left hand and mashed it good. It wouldn't have been such a nagging injury, the doctor scolded when I finally saw her, if I hadn't tried to play four holes of golf a few days later.

In my defense, I would have quit on the first painful swing but it hit the fairway and before I knew it I parred the darn hole. What self-respecting hacker would pick up after that?

Anyway, I can handle an extra-long Big Wait. I've been waiting since June for my so-called friends to prove their friendship and send me a golf shirt or sleeve of balls.

This goes way back to when, within one week's time, two chain letters arrived. One was from Fred, an old friend who lives in Atlanta, which I now understand is about the right distance for running this scam. He told of a new golf shirt game that was sweeping the country and if I would only send one shirt from any course to the person at the top of the enclosed list – his dad, by the way – I would be rewarded 36-fold in a matter of weeks. It was tempting – enough shirts to clothe the Nike Tour and it would only cost me one.

"This is not a chain letter," he said in closing, which is also what it said in the letter on my desk later that week, this one from an editor telling of a new game sweeping the country and if I would just send one sleeve of golf balls to the person at the top of the list ...

The person at the top of the list was my boss, the big boss who pays me for such things as sitting at my desk reading ski tips on slow days.

Would Maxflis do?

Trusting that she will never read this confession – and trusting none of you will tell her – I will admit that the Maxflis were a Christmas gift anyway so I was out nothing. But I did stop at a discount golf shop, buy a $10 shirt with a nice logo and ship it off to Fred's dad, and I did spend a couple hours sending my own requests to friends at work and across the state. Chain letters or not, no way I would be the missing link.

As I said, that was June. And I am still waiting. My so-called friends laughed at the letters or averted their eyes when I entered the room. One friend said sorry, chain letters were illegal; this from a man who rolls the ball over during summer rules. Others simply snorted in disbelief when they saw me, like I was too stupid to know these things never work.

Yeah? I replied. Well, read this:

"Thanks for the golf shirt," wrote Fred's dad. "It was certainly thoughtful of you ... "

I've about given up, but as long as it's the Big Wait for spring, I'll wait a bit longer for shirts and balls.

Meanwhile, this advice: Many injuries could be avoided with good pre-ski conditioning.

Maybe a check of priorities
is needed now and then

July 1993

If and when they get the new all-golf cable channel fired up and on the air (was there really a demand for this?), I hope they do reruns. I'd like to see again a sultry autumn evening in Milwaukee in 1991 when Calvin Peete, the old straight-shooter, took a bunch of kids out for a lesson.

The muckety-mucks of the golf world were all at a fancy banquet that night. It was the week of the Greater Milwaukee Open, defending champion Greg Norman was the center of attention and everybody who was anybody was at the fancy Pfister Hotel to celebrate.

Just about everybody. Out at modest little Lincoln Park GC, a nine-hole county course that hugs the Milwaukee River and separates the city from its suburbs, two-time GMO winner Peete had eschewed the fancy banquet to advance the work of his Minority Youth Golf Foundation.

The man who once earned a living selling goods to field workers from the trunk of his car believed that golf and business were inextricably linked, and if black and other minority youngsters are to compete on an equal basis in business someday, they could do worse than to know about golf and its rules. So while the powers-that-be were dining downtown, Peete was explaining the power-that-*could*-be to several hundred kids and adults.

Get a good grip, he told them. Keep your eye on the ball, always. Avoid trouble by going where the traps weren't. Stay straight.

He told them about golf, too, about how after he became successful in the game he went back to school and earned his high school diploma. Ever the straight shooter.

I thought about Peete when they recently announced the all-golf cable channel, an Arnold Palmer-backed project which could be on the air in 1994, carrying a handful of PGA tournaments, the Nike Tour, instruction, travel stories and more.

And I thought about Peete again when I heard about other recent breakthroughs for golf, such as something called the Celebrity Golf Association, which plans to expand its Hollywood-soaked tournament schedule from five events in 1993 to 10 next year, and the new Pro Athletes Golf League, starring overpaid 7-handicappers in nail-biting competition for purses the LPGA would feel lucky to get.

Some of these great events might be found on the all-golf channel, but it's even worse than that. Others, including a $400,000 celebrity tournament in July, will be on network TV.

Golf today is rich as Croesus. Going into the U.S. Open, 44 PGA players had already earned more than $200,000 in prize money this year and that doesn't begin to count corporate Mondays, club and clothing endorsements or the fall made-for-TV tournaments that pour ever greater sums on those who already made the most all year.

Golf has even followed baseball's path (and shouldn't that give us all pause) by establishing fantasy camps, such as one in Las Vegas that will carry a $25,000 per camper price tag.

That includes a bag tag, no doubt.

So golf is going just great, it seems. Taken together, all these developments suggest that in its latest explosion this great game knows no bounds.

Or, some might say, shame. What's next? Demolition golf? Funniest golf videos?

The one thing you won't find is Calvin Peete's Minority Youth Golf Foundation, which he had to give up on last fall due to lack of corporate support. While Coca-Cola, IBM, the PGA Tour and a few others helped out, he said it was financially impossible to conduct a national schedule of clinics such as the one in Lincoln Park that night.

"It saddens me deeply," he told *Golf World* magazine. "Golf, with its honor system, is such a character-building sport, an excellent outlet" for inner city kids.

It saddens me too, that in this game there is support for televised competition between celebrities and athletes but not enough for constructive efforts like Peete's. Sometime soon couch-bound golf fans will be able to thrill to the drama of a handsomely rewarded second-string quarterback standing over a $40,000 4-foot putt at Lake Tahoe while eager sponsors watch at green's edge.

Golf, the industry, may be richer for that. Golf, the game, will be poorer.

Author's Note: Obviously there was a demand for an all-golf cable channel. I watch The Golf Channel all the time.

A Scottish heritage
(plus Cindy Crawford)

Winter 1997

It was Tom Kennen's charge to add a back nine to Tagalong GC on beautiful Red Cedar Lake, nine new holes of golf in the tradition of Tagalong's 75-year-old front nine. So it was the logical question: Did you send to Scotland for the grass seed, I asked, and for the men to spread it?

Nae, he said, nae.

"Not this time."

Not, he was saying, like last time.

Rich men have built golf courses in Wisconsin since the game was first brought here, but the story of Tagalong GC in Barron County is as much a testament to wealth as you'll find. It was built in the 1920s by a man who had not merely a summer home in northwestern Wisconsin but an entire summer island, a refuge on which he spent well over $1 million in the days when a dollar was still a dollar, not just less than the price of a water-salvaged Titleist.

F.D. Stout was a director of the Chicago, St. Paul and Omaha Railroad in the years after the turn of the century and, not coincidentally, one of the wealthiest men in Chicago. Shortly after the turn of the century he purchased half-interest in a small island in Red Cedar Lake where he built a hunting shack and, later, a log home.

Not just any log home, however. Stout wanted a summer place in the style of those sprawling Adirondack resorts, and so he built himself one.

He sent to Idaho for the best cedar logs and brought in carpenters who were

ordered only to move them in winter, when they could be hauled across snow without scarring. The floors were 4-inch planks of carved stone from Italy and other materials were from Germany. There were separate houses for children and quarters for nursemaids and butlers, and when he was done he stuck an iron plate at the threshold proclaiming it "The Isle of Happy Days."

Then he decided he wanted a golf course. Do you think he would have been satisfied mowing the nearby pasture?

Stout picked out land on the mainland, a short boat trip from his island. The land had to be cleared of stumps, of course, and Stout's son, Allison, later recalled that a man called "Dynamite" Oftedahl was responsible for blasting away many stumps and rocks.

But Stout didn't want a cleared field with flags. That was no golf course. He wanted a course inspired by the legendary St. Andrews, so he sent to Scotland for seed and the men to put it in, and he ordered a course built in the links style. Stone buildings that served as pump house and waiting shelter at the lake – then, as now, access was by boat from the island – were roofed with sawed cedar shingles for a thatched look. The course featured open fairways, elevated greens, deep grass bunkers and little mounds here and there.

"I think they called them chocolate drops back in the '20s and '30s," said Kennen, whose parents, Bud and Jackie, now own the course. Tom and his brothers, Scott and Dennis, are all involved.

Adding nine holes to that kind of storied course wasn't easy. Architects wanted to rebuild the original nine to obtain more room for the new holes but the Kennens didn't want to disrupt Stout's work. The alternative, however, was to build new holes on land that didn't provide as much space as Stout's builder had enjoyed.

"A lot of work," Kennen said. "I think I spent about 400 hours one winter, redesigning holes and deciding how to go. It was a big responsibility, actually, not to ruin the character of the old course."

The new Tagalong will blend new holes and old for a par-71 layout. The new nine will open by July if all goes well, in time for guests at Stout's old summer home – now Stout's Lodge, a fine inn and conference center – to come by boat for a round of golf. The new Tagalong won't be St. Andrews, it won't even be Stout's dream, but occasionally the glamour of wealth and fame will shine through again.

"Jeez, last year we even had Cindy Crawford come over and play golf," Kennen said. "Boy, that was an exciting day. We were all watching her."

The Isle of Happy Days, indeed.

Combining camaraderie
and golf since 1934

September 2004

The great writer and golfer John Updike once declared that "solitary golf is barren fun," that the camaraderie of the game was as essential as the swing.

"Golf is a game of the mind and soul as much as of the muscles," he wrote, "and without companionship as pointless as a one-man philosophical symposium."

Some of us who play solo golf early in the morning or who haunt the last shadows of the evening to squeeze in a round might quibble, but Updike has a point. Sometimes, in fact, the camaraderie becomes as important as the golf, which explains why Florence Migacz will be on hand in October when the Grant Park Women's 18-hole Golf Club celebrates its 70th anniversary with a banquet, program, commemorative 1934-2004 towels and, it can be expected, much reminiscing.

At 91, Migacz doesn't play golf anymore; the body has a way of saying enough is enough. But the club has been a part of her life since, "Well, let's see, since 1943," she said.

Pause.

"It's a long time."

And that's good for some memories. When she joined the club many of the women didn't have cars so they would carry their clubs onto streetcars, get off at a stop near Grant Park on Milwaukee County's south side and walk the rest of the way to the course. They carried their clubs to play, as well, because it wasn't until later that rolling carts would be available and even later than that before motorized carts – would you look at that! – came along.

"None of the ladies wore pants at that time," Migacz said. "We wore skirts and blouses." Not to mention skirts with slips that on warm days would get damp and stick to their legs. "It's much easier with the clothes we have nowadays," she said.

Those were good times. Sometimes the county staff would have workers pick berries so fresh pies could be served in the lakeside clubhouse after the round, and there were more social events and on-course games every week. The club championship was a bigger deal than it is now, she said; many of the members would go out and walk the 36-hole final match to see the outcome firsthand.

It is different now. The social part has taken a backseat to golf first, in Migacz's view. People are so busy today they don't have time for all that, and of course there are more courses competing for players so numbers aren't what they were either.

"And many of those friends I had have a golf club in their hands up in heaven, watching us," she said.

Jane Polasek, who is the current club president, said there are still members who come for the Sheepshead card games that follow, as much as the golf itself, not that the game isn't important. The club championship in August is still a big deal.

But – and here come echoes of Updike – Polasek said she joined three years ago for the chance to play more golf and got even more for her money.

"I think it's the camaraderie. You make friends. For me it's been nice. A lot of the women who are friends of mine don't play golf. I would always wind up playing with the men, and a lot of the men were big slicers or hookers and I would always end up walking down the fairway by myself."

Barren fun, that. Happy anniversary.

My dream foursome

November 1999

There is a picture on my basement wall that raises one of the great questions in golf, on a par with such cosmic puzzlements as "What 10 records would you take to a desert island?" and "One night only – Ginger or Mary Ann?"

The photograph is from a tournament several years ago – I think it was the Masters where Tiger Woods announced there was a new sheriff in town – and shows the youngster watching one of his booming drives disappear into the distance. His partners that day, standing behind Woods wearing looks of awe and age, were Arnold Palmer and Jack Nicklaus.

Three of golf's greatest generations on one tee. Wouldn't it have been awesome to be the fourth in that group?

And that's the question I've been posing lately. If you could play with any three people – dead, alive, golfers or nongolfers – who would they be? The sky is the limit. Name your dream foursome.

My neighbor Reg, who was checking the oil in his car when I popped the question, followed his interest in military history. He would tee it up with Dwight Eisenhower, Douglas MacArthur and George S. Patton because he has read their biographies and admires their careers. (It also would complement his tendancy toward – right, left, right, left – army golf.)

Eisenhower would have a busy day. Gerald Boyle, the defense attorney, would play with Ike, John Kennedy and Ronald Reagan. "The three of them were great statesmen (and) they're all good golfers, you know," he said. "I would just like to be an observer. I'm sure that the conversation would be unbelievably fascinating."

Paul Gossens, another lawyer, also thinks "the 19th hole conversation would be the best in the world" with his dream team of Jesus Christ, Muhammad and Buddha. But the Nassau could be complicated. "I wonder what their handicaps would be?" he said.

Barry Hansen, the golf pro at Apostle Highlands GC in Bayfield, would honor his joint connections to Texas and Wisconsin, and the biggest influences on his game. "Well, Harvey Penick for me," he said. "And then Ben Crenshaw and Manuel de la Torre."

I was actually on the first tee one day when I asked my partner Dan who he would rather be with. Michael Jordan, he said, because he's Michael. Bill Clinton, just to see if he could really shoot 84 without a dozen mulligans. "And my dad, (who is 89) because he can't play anymore and those were some of the best times of my life."

My friend Tim went the same route. "My dad, because I never got to. Ben Crenshaw, because I think he'd have some pretty interesting stories. And David Feherty, because like everybody else I like a funny Irishman."

Some who weighed the question started down Serious Street for a few blocks before turning left onto Fantasy Avenue, which is fine. Jay the payroll man in my office would play with Arnold Palmer and Sam Snead, because they are Arnold Palmer and Sam Snead, while the fourth – because hope is golf's middle name – would be Jan Stephenson. "We're the same age," he said, like that would help.

My neighbor Joel started with Bill Murray and Groucho Marx – "for laughs" – and finished with Jamie Lee Curtis. Not for laughs, I suspect. At least, his wife didn't. Even my own wife would take to the first tee Nancy Lopez, her longtime role model, the long-hitting Laura Davies and someone named Greg Norman. For his golf, she explained.

U.S. Bank Championship tournament director Dan Croak would stick with golfers, but it wasn't an easy choice. "I suppose I'd have to say Ben Hogan, and Tiger Woods. Hmmm. And Fred Couples. Love his attitude ... I just would like to spend four hours in his company."

Others had a hard time limiting themselves to a foursome. Bob the sportswriter chose Sam Snead and Arnold Palmer, then threw in Ben Hogan because he grew up playing Hogan clubs. Then he realized he'd never even thought to include a woman, and forgot his father altogether. Beverly the bookseller had the same problem. She chose Arnold Palmer, for obvious reasons, Fred Couples, because she just adores him, and Sam Snead, because she has tried to follow his book of instruction for 100 years and maybe in person his ideas would kick in. But then she wanted Nancy Lopez, too, and Jenny Chuasiriporn and ...

Beverly, I said, no fivesomes.

See how tough it is? As for me, I'd like Arnie and maybe Chi Chi.

But I'm going with a priest, a minister and a rabbi. With all those celebrities on the course, we're going to need some jokes during backups.

Dubious decision on
an all-important 'stroke'

November 2002

I f golf has a Hot Stove League, here's one worth telling on those long, cold winter nights.

Craig Beyers and Aaron Feldman had a longstanding tradition. Two of them, actually. When they teed it up this summer in Ozaukee CC's important member-guest invitational tourney, The Oz, it marked their 14th straight appearance as a team.

And their failure-to-win streak – in truth more of a never-came-close streak – stood at 13.

But maybe more than in any other game hope springs eternal in golf, so the two friends waded bravely into competition once more and on the tournament's second day found themselves – can you believe it? – in contention. As preliminary play was winding down, they were in position for the first time ever to qualify for the tournament's eight-team, three-hole championship playoff when – and can you believe this, either? – Feldman noticed he had a problem.

"Aaron said that his vision seemed a little blurred or fuzzy and he was having trouble seeing," Beyers said.

Or, as Feldman put it, "I ended up with double vision, which is rather difficult to play golf with. I was seeing two of everything, so when I'd stand over the golf ball there would be two golf balls there."

It was scary, of course. Beyers suggested they pull out and get Feldman checked, but his stalwart partner would have none of that. He felt certain the

double vision was the result of a new blood pressure medication he had started the day before, nothing to force him to pull out of a playoff he and Beyers
had finally achieved after all those years.

"Absolutely not, we're not going to stop, I'll be fine," Feldman insisted.
Beyers tried to tell Feldman it was in his best interest to stop playing and get
attention, but Feldman said no. Beyers could go in if he wanted but, double
vision or not, he was playing on.

"Of course we were all concerned and wanted to quit, and of course he didn't
want to have any part of that," said Beyers. "He wasn't going to let anything
stop his participation in the event."

Not that stubborn determination cleared up his vision. When he looked
down he would still see two balls, and he could only swing at one.

"He said, 'Which is it?' " said Beyers. "And he did say 'Can you point to it?'
So I did take the club and point to it and he said, 'Now I see two club shafts.'
You couldn't point to one and say that's the one."

Deep inside, Feldman said later, he "sort of" figured his problem was something more serious than the medication but "I guess it wasn't as important as
playing in the tournament."

Feldman's strategy was to blink a lot, close one eye during address to try to
eliminate the wrong target "and just give it a whack and see what happened."
Amazingly, on the first playoff hole he hit as fine a drive as he could imagine,
220 yards or so, and their team got a par while most of their competitors
scored 6s or 7s.

The next hole was a long, hard par-4 with a three-tiered, tightly-cut green
and, to bring them back to earth a bit, they trudged off with a 7. But on the
third and last playoff hole, a par-3, they managed a bogey that was good
enough for the win. Carl the greenskeeper couldn't come up with a better
Cinderella story.

"It was really Craig that did it," Feldman told me later, which seems too
modest an explanation. Craig couldn't have played the alternate-shot format
himself, could he? Feldman didn't stay for the dinner, deciding it finally
might be time to go rest, and though he was feeling much better by Monday
he did go see his doctor.

The diagnosis was "a very minor, little episode," he said, which in lay terms
we would call a small stroke. (Strokes, like heart attacks or flesh wounds, are

only minor when they happen to someone else.)

For their trouble they won a fine trophy modeled after a statue on the club grounds. And Feldman said he is fine now as well, with no aftereffects. When he looks at the trophy, which he does often, he doesn't see two.

"It was fun," he now says. "And of course the trophy at the end made it all worthwhile."

So the scary story has a happy ending, but it may still serve as a cautionary tale for other golfers.

Be careful what you wish for, friends. When you go to the first tee and demand strokes, be very, very specific.

Dawn 'til dusk on Wisconsin's 'Gangster Tour'

September 2005

I have a friend who would no sooner play just nine holes of golf than confess to fudging on his taxes. For him, half a round is merely foreplay without fruition.

I have another friend who only plays nine holes at a time. For him the appetizer is banquet enough.

I play with both, but generally speaking I'm a more-golf-the-merrier kind of guy. I sometimes regret that the old goatherds who built St. Andrews didn't leave behind a 24-hole track, or even more, for the rest of the world to copy. If we must suffer an eight-hour work day, why not eight hours of golf at a time?

But some days less is more, or at least enough. I was thinking that recently when, after driving more than four hours on critically important newspaper business, or possibly a lark, I arrived at my destination, little Miscauno Island in the Menominee River in Marinette County, home to a century-old resort and the only slightly younger Four Seasons GC.

Claiming four seasons of golf in far northern Wisconsin is pretty amusing, but it's a fine little par-34 layout that I've played a few times. I once wrote that it was one of those rare golf courses where you could hook a drive into one state or slice it into another – and from the same tee, though unless you have a Paul Bunyanesque slice it's probably not true. But that day when I climbed from my car it offered the perfect tonic for a road-weary golfer.

For a little island, Miscauno has a lot of history. The first resort, called

Miscauno Inn, opened in 1905, built by the Wisconsin and Michigan Railroad to entertain the swells of Chicago. On the night its doors were thrown open, special trains brought hundreds of celebrants from the lumber towns of Marinette, Peshtigo and Menominee to join the "prominent Chicago people" who were guests of the railroad.

The Peshtigo Times called it "the greatest social event in the area's history" at "the equal of the most exclusive clubs in Chicago." That was Oct. 9, 1905. In December, one of its founders, John R. Walsh of Chicago, met financial ruin when his railroad, mining and banking empire collapsed, and he later went to prison.

A bad omen, I'd say, and it was. The original inn lasted until the 1920s, surviving the winter when thieves arrived on big sleighs and gutted the place of furnishings, until fire consumed it. Two years later it was rebuilt and opened as the Four Seasons Club; the golf course was added and it began to operate as a private club for wealthy Chicagoans. Much later it had several different owners, until in 1998 it was seized by the federal government after its then-owners, Cicero, Ill., town president Betty Loren-Maltese and other mob-connected figures, were charged with buying and improving the resort with money embezzled in an insurance scam.

Just another reason there was often an illicit whisper about the place. Like most resorts in northern Wisconsin back then, it offered casino games (the first time I visited in the 1990s there were still gambling devices in storage upstairs) and it has long been rumored that Al Capone was among its guests. A later owner who doubles as island historian insists Capone was never there, but the whisper of such names never hurts advertising. Even today the resort's new owners, who have added a beautiful new 55-room all-suite hotel for the island's 100th year in the hospitality business, drop Capone's name in their brochure.

"Shadowed by recently questionable ties to Chicago's underground," the brochure says, "its mysterious past has done little to taint the glorious appeal of the Four Seasons Club ... "

It's not the only Wisconsin golf course with such ties. In Winter, in Sawyer County, Barker Lake GC similarly has Chicago gangster roots, this time owing to its early ownership by one Joe "Polack Joe" Saltis, a Joliet saloon keeper and bootlegger who was said to have been a fearsome competitor.

Saltis had dirt brought in from Tennessee to build his course on a wide spot in the Chippewa River. It has been reported that no one in Sawyer County was fooled by the hotel workers whose weapons were hardly the sort for Wisconsin hunting. But Saltis threw around a bit of green and everybody got along well, even after a game warden named Ernie Swift slipped by Saltis' boys and arrested the bootlegger for fishing too close to the Winter dam.

I was thinking about Saltis the next morning when I awoke on Miscauno Island, again facing a long day's drive, which I immediately decided could wait until I attempted nine short drives of another sort. And so it did.

When I got home, as luck would have it, an e-mail had arrived from a friend who had recently hit upon a brainstorm while playing nine holes of golf at three different courses near his northern Wisconsin cabin in one day. If nine holes at three courses was fun, he wrote, why not try for five? His thinking is that on a long June day a man could tee it up for nine at Gateway GC in Land O' Lakes at 7 a.m. and proceed from there to four other courses in and around Eagle River for nine holes each. He would finish at Plum Lake GC in Sayner, where he would "start the nightcap nine at around 7, and still have sufficient light to play the bell hole coming home."

"Interested?" he asked.

Are you kidding? Does a bear sleep in the woods?

Just nine holes. Five times. I bet Al Capone never did that.

My kingdom, my rules

November 2003

U h-oh. I've been thinking.

Arnold Palmer is "The King of Golf" and always will be, and until that far-off day when he lands in that big bunker in the sky – the one no man can get out of, swing wild as he may – the job will be his.

But I've been thinking when the throne is open, I would sure like to be next. No, not THAT throne, wise guy.

The top job, the one that comes with a crown. I'm not sure exactly how one goes about applying to be king, but with a little tinkering here and some tightening there I could do great things for golf in MY kingdom.

In my kingdom tee times would always be available, the season would begin on March 1, even in Wisconsin, and no course could demand your credit card just to hold a tee time. I hate giving strangers my credit card number over the phone.

Besides, you'll have cash enough. In my kingdom you would not have to cough up $100 or $150 or – yikes – $200 or more to play golf when $50 or $75 is more than enough to pay for four hours of self-punishment. Think of it this way: A plumber charges $40 an hour to fix our toilet and we scream in outrage, so why should a golf course charge more than that per hour to play a simple game? If we're worried about growing the game, let's ungrow the cost.

Of course, courses currently charging usurious green fees would want to be grandfathered. Fine.

But did you ever notice that the more a course charges for golf, the more it also charges for a souvenir cap that only serves as free advertising anyway? What's with that? So here's the deal – in my kingdom, any course charging more than $100 has to throw a hat in, too.

Without rules the game would be anarchy, so let's have them. But no more stroke AND distance for a ball out of bounds. Losing a good ball is punishment in itself, so under my system it will be stroke OR distance. You choose.

Penalties are important, though. So in my kingdom that guy in your group – you know which one, the guy who is always fluffing it up in the rough or playing winter rules in the bunker – could be whacked in the knee with an 8-iron for every violation.

Also, any couch slug who watches golf on television and calls the network to tattle a rules violation – like the one that cost Paul Azinger two strokes because his caddie pulled the flag a second early, not that any of the players noticed – would be assessed a two-shot penalty in his next round for failing to have a life.

In my kingdom, no golf shirt would cost $129, like ones I saw recently. It won't make your game any better than a $49 model, and do you really think the poor Sri Lankan who made it cares if you spent $129 on it?

Ooh, just thought of this. Any course charging $200 for a round has to throw in a $129 shirt.

A guy told me recently he took his father to a very popular and highly regarded Wisconsin course and paid $50 each for a round of golf, only to find the greens had not only just been aerated, but the plugs were still on the green. It was like putting on a cribbage board – with the pegs in.

No way. Playing a course without good greens is playing half a course, and full price should never be charged.

Same with temporary tees. Give a golfer the whole course or give him a break.

Mandatory caddies, not mandatory carts.

I could accept cheaper fees for seniors, but let's tweak that one a bit. In my kingdom you would get the break not for the age you are, but for the age you look. (This was inspired by an incident the other day when I heard a young whippersnapper outside a public restroom I was using say, "Come on, old man, hurry up." So sure, it's self-serving, but that's what kings do.)

Any player who can't lock his car in the parking lot without honking the horn for all to hear would lose two strokes before he even reaches the tee. That has nothing to do with golf, unless the honk is in someone's backswing. It just really annoys me.

Now we're rolling. If you have a 12:10 p.m. tee time and the guy in the clubhouse announces, "Well, we're running 20 minutes behind," you play for free. But these things run both ways. If you make a 12:10 tee time and arrive at 12:18 expecting someone to cart you out to your group, you'll pay for the ride. Dearly.

And if you make a tee time and don't show, costing someone else a chance to play and taking money from the course owner's pocket, he will be entitled to come into your house and take money from yours. Fair is only fair.

No cell phones could be used except to report heart attacks. Not little grabbers, either. Only the big one.

It's only right your playing partners be allowed to call in a new fourth.

On patrol with the Geese Police

July 2005

I should point out right at the get-go that I don't hate all geese.

Mother Goose could spin a pretty good yarn. The Watertown Goslings got their name from an odd but interesting era when Watertown stuffed geese were a highly-sought delicacy. And there's still a bit of a rush in watching the first geese of the season migrating overhead, north or south, according to a calendar we can't understand.

That's the key, though. Migrating geese know when to get the flock out of here, not like those detestable resident geese who in recent years have invaded our golf courses and parks and ponds and fouled them with – well, let Dianne Neveras handle the specifics.

"Each goose leaves a pound and a half of droppings a day," she said, just getting warmed up. "Seven and a half minutes from bill to butt.

"Don't ask me who timed it."

Doesn't matter. We who play on fields and fairways know too well that however many minutes from bill to butt, it's four hours of nuisance or more walking around it, preferably, or through it, disgustingly. That's why it's good to hear that for resident geese in Wisconsin, there's a new sheriff in town.

The Geese Police. And it's a K-9 unit.

Geese Police began on the East Coast in 1986, Neveras said, when founder and now president Dave Marcks was working at a golf course in Connecticut. Thanks to pesky geese, it wasn't always glamorous work.

"He was the guy with the shovel standing behind them picking up after the geese," said Neveras, "and he said there has to be a better way."

There was. Marcks began using a trained Border collie to herd the geese and disrupt their nesting, a treatment that proved successful at the course where he worked at the time.

Once the geese were gone, though, he had a bored dog. Then someone who knew of his work asked Marcks to help him rid a property of geese, and suddenly Marcks became aware there was opportunity to be seized. Like making lemons into lemonade – or, more fitting here, poop into pâté – Marcks saw a way to profit from this common nuisance, and Geese Police was born. Today he has 37 working Border collies in his New Jersey operation, along with franchises in several states, including Wisconsin, said Neveras, who is vice president and director of franchise operations.

The president of the Wisconsin franchise is Susan Kinney, who heard about Geese Police when she applied for a job as dog handler for the Illinois franchise. The owner didn't need an additional employee, but Kinney was so intrigued by what she learned about the company that she moved to Whitewater from Illinois with her husband and son and bought the southern Wisconsin franchise. It's going so well, she said, that already they have added a third dog to the two that came with the franchise package.

Border collies make the best Geese Police because of their herding technique (think of the movie "Babe" but without the pig) and for the way they give geese "the eye." While the dogs do not touch the birds – wildlife officials would view that as a no-no – the geese see the dogs as predators and leave the area. For golf courses, it's best to get the dogs active early in the season before nesting can begin.

"Once they have the goslings, they're there. You're stuck with them then," said Kinney, whose crew includes Kirt, Top and Smut, as in Smut the Mutt. While treatment programs vary according to the number of geese and other factors, some clients have extreme problems. One golf course that called them last season had so many resident geese that they were landing on the fairway even as the dogs were rousting others. They were there for eight hours the first day and long hours after that, but course members were eventually free of birds.

"They were thrilled," Kinney said. "We started that one real early again this year."

In addition to golf courses, Geese Police clients include cemeteries (it really has to be a nuisance to bother the dead), corporate parks with ponds, condo projects and wherever else grasslands and water lure resident flocks. Not to turn this into a commercial, but if you are looking for a new career, franchise fees start at about $35,000, including two dogs, plus other startup expenses that put the get-started cost at between $50,000 and $100,000, Neveras said.

Additional dogs run about $5,000 on average, she said. That's a lot, considering you'll need to keep them in Kibbles and Bits thereafter, but given the number of goslings I saw on a course the very day I spoke with Neveras and Kinney, multiplied by a pound and a half a day, you'll probably never have to worry about job security. Unless some legislators decide to offer a hunting season for golf course geese instead of those nice feral cats, someone will be needed to turn that poop into pâté.

"That's what Dave keeps saying," Neveras said. "(He says) 'I can't believe I stepped in it – literally.' "

Good friends,
dubious golf ... perfect!

July 2000

One of the great things about golf is the tradition that is the game's heart and soul.

But not all of it takes place on the course. Some of it hangs at the edges, like the gallery, where it is no less enjoyable for its supporting role. I drove for three hours the other day to play a round of golf with friends of many years' standing in an event that has become a rite for us all. Funny thing, though. While the golf is still the come-on in the invitation, the gathering has assumed an importance all its own.

Maybe, if we're honest, it's become the point.

Of course, having just observed the annual declaration of handicaps, honesty isn't a big concern.

It began in the early 1980s when a group of us who loosely worked together in Madison began traveling one day each spring to Stevens Point to play golf with friends there, who later instituted a return match each fall.

Any good tradition is built of habits stacked like bricks. In the early years, we would pile into one player's motor home and play poker all the way north (a practice that sadly ended when he retired to that big first tee in the sky) and would stop for heavy slabs of pre-lunch pie in Westfield. Now we travel in several cars and pay more attention to diet. Not to mention that some found coconut cream curdles in gin.

But other habits run on like an overheated putt. New players have come and some have gone but the core remains remarkably intact. As always, lunch began with the ceremonial telling of jokes, which this year featured appearances by Ray Charles and Tiger Woods, Cardinal Jack Nicklaus and Rabbi Tiger Woods, a rich man in a Cadillac, the Pope, a woman on her way to a nymphomaniac convention in Chicago and Pablo Kowalski. Please know that the Pope and the woman on her way to Chicago were in different jokes.

As always, Bob the Voluble had us on the edge of our seats while he henscratched on a scrap of paper to come up with pairings. The anticipation was not over who would win; Bob the Voluble's group somehow wins every year. The mystery was over how he would screw the teams up, and he did not disappoint. After 20 minutes of ciphering he announced three foursomes and one threesome that he declared the most balanced in all his years of making pairings.

Of course, that was because he included one player twice and me not at all. The man is one tax audit away from Waupun. It took an actuary a few seats down the table to get the job done.

Next came rules, few of which Frank Hannigan would recognize. There would be one mulligan a side; even par-3s would be eligible for second chances. Those over 70 years of age or with handicaps above 25 could elect to use the forward tees. And one player moved that no more than two putts should be scored on 18, because everyone should go away happy. It was unanimous. If someone had moved that we all take a 75 and head for the bar it likely would have passed, but no one did so we went off to play golf.

It was, as always, great fun, never mind that morning sunshine vanished as we approached the tee and the afternoon was filled with scuttering dark clouds and a soundtrack of rumble thunder escorted us all the way. Occasionally it spattered raindrops and the wind blew but in short it was a beautiful day for golf, filled with the usual high highs and low misery this game embodies.

Later there was dinner, a more formal affair than in the early years, featuring wine now and actual forks. It was so civilized that some spouses joined us for the meal and no one told stories about nymphomaniacs. Then came dessert, and departures.

It wasn't like Champions Dinner at the Masters, I'm sure, but in its way it was a day of tradition and fellowship that I wouldn't have missed. We are men of different backgrounds and politics (from a one-time Pentagon official to a one-time conscientious objector) brought together by the magnet that is golf and held there by the glue that is friendship. Yes, the game has been good to us.

Oh, who won? I don't recall exactly, except that two teams tied and I wasn't on either. In the preliminary match, it was Rabbi Woods over Cardinal Nicklaus by three strokes.

Golf or love ...
it's all the same game

October 1994

Not to be a braggart, but I would like to close out this season with the story of how at last I beat the devil at his own cursed game.

And what a story. How after years of hard work and heartbreak I broke my driver the way a cowboy breaks a wild bronc, how I wrestled my putter for control and won and how after a series of tragic near-misses finally played the round of my life, a sparkling 79 that will long live in clubhouse lore.

In the wind yet, and rain.

Yeah, raining like a son of a ...

Aw, you're on to me. Truth is, when I finally got close I three-putted 17 and 18 for nothing like a 79, so we're left to ponder instead a riddle posed during a late-season round at a county course in Milwaukee.

Golf, or women?

My friend and I were teamed with two strangers, one a veteran, the other new to the game. He had taken it up only in April and was self-taught, he said, but pretty competent for one still learning to crawl, golf-wise. Between shots he practiced his setup and swing. He putted out on every hole, not wanting to cheat himself by picking up a 2-footer. He didn't own a car, he said, and stored his clubs in a locker at the course so he could ride his bike over almost every day to play.

This was truly a man smitten.

"This is what I live for now," he said as we walked up a fairway.

Yes, I commiserated, golf is a lot like heroin. Just more expensive.

I was kidding, but he wasn't.

"I like it better than women," he said, as serious as a 4-footer for birdie.

"I can't handle women anymore."

I don't remember saying anything back. I mean, I understand a guy taking a marital mulligan, and if he hooks that one out of bounds as well I don't object to reaching for a whole new sleeve.

But really, you can't handle women so you take up golf?

This is what they call a difference without a distinction.

When you think about it, as I did for the rest of that round, golf and love are so similar you'd think Pete Dye designed them both.

Take it from a guy whose wife got him another woman for Valentine's Day. (Name of Bertha, if you must know, and I don't mean my wife.) Golf is the ultimate metaphor for the game started by the first twosome, Adam and Eve, who strayed from the fairway into everlasting rough.

Each can be maddening, exhilirating, fun, painful, frustrating, rewarding and near-suicide-inducing, all on the same day. Just when you think you've had it up to here with the whole business, something good will happen to bring you back, all the bad stuff erased from life's card. It's much the same game.

Don't you believe me? Try this: Find a single golf cliche or common term that couldn't also apply to matters of the heart, such as, "The saddest words in golf are, 'You're still away.'"

Same with love.

Or, "Hey, would you like to play around?"

And of course, "Never up, never ... "

Er, mind.

But the resemblances roll on. Each is a game that some take to as naturally as if they were born to it while others need a little help in the technique department. The bookshelves are filled with instruction in each. Magazines offer advice, sometimes with pictures! Some people even need videos to get going. And there is an army of counselors for those who find themselves struggling.

"Harvey Penick's Little Red Book" is Xaviera Hollander's little black one. Jack Nicklaus is Dr. Ruth without the accent.

And if you take it one step farther, just about every hint for better performance is as useful at Hawthorne Hills as in the honeymoon suite.

A little warm-up is always best. Slow down there, Speedo, this isn't a race. Always keep your left arm straight.

I should have told the poor fellow on the day we played, but he'll learn soon enough. As Dr. Ruth said to Harvey Penick, it doesn't mean a thing if you ain't got the swing.

Had an ace? Tell the world

March 2001

A few years ago my voluble friend Chuck got a hole-in-one, but maybe you knew that. He told everyone but the parish priest and now that I think of it he was in the confessional a rather long time. It got so that after one round I announced to everyone in the bar that Chuck had had an ace, just to save his voice.

If he gets one this year, no such problem. All he'll have to do is tap a few computer keys and his hole-in-one will have, as one online Hole-In-One Registry put it, "World Wide fame." As Cudahy's Gary Hafemann told the world after his ace at Oakwood GC last July, "What a great feeling!!!!!" With, yes, five exclamation points. Donald Williams of Beaver Dam needed only two to tell the story of his ace last summer, but in the cyber grill room there is little holding back.

The hole-in-one is a funny thing. Most golfers will never get one, but it is a remarkably common thing. The Web site www.nothingbutgolf.com estimates the odds for the average golfer on any one hole at 33,000-to-1, yet the hole-in-one fairy visits thousands of golfers every season, many of whom turn immediately to the Internet to spread the news.

As in any 19th hole, some in the cyber grill will tell you more than you wanted to know. "The pin was at the back on the two-tier green that runs at a 45-degree angle from the tee ... " read one exhaustive posting. Michael Annunziata of Highland Lakes, Ill., similarly shared too much information by screaming, "MY FIRST HOLE-IN-ONE WAS THE BEST FEELING I EVER HAD BESIDES SEX." But others, like Fond du Lac's Gary Wild, keep it simple.

"Titleist 962, 5-iron, Pinnacle LS golf ball," he said. The swing, of course, was all his. Or take golfer D. Stock of Baldwin, who used a just-the-facts ma'am style in reporting his September ace at Badlands GC to the World Wide Hole-In-One Club at www.sunnygolf.com.

"Charity golf tourney; 9 beers; 3 witnesses; in on the fly; still finished second; won 28 bucks; had to buy more beer."

Others don't hide the excitement, though. "Overcome with joy, I sprinted the entire 161 yards to make sure my eyes were not decieving me," Eagle's Dustin Deal reported after his lucky shot at Evergreen GC last May.

Paul Kramer of Milwaukee, who won a Harley for his ace at a charity event at Country Club of Wisconsin in July, admitted, "After two, three seconds of utter disbelief we let out a collective roar that would have made the King of the Jungle proud." And Antigo's Paul Galuska, who aced on Sept. 17 at Riverview GC, said, "Voice became extremely sore after screaming and yelling for at least 2 minutes."

Still others stress their hole-in-one came from skillful golf, not dumb luck. Alan Perry of Oak Creek paraphrased Snoopy's "dark and stormy night" in describing the conditions he overcame by writing, "It was a cold and windy day for October ... " And Todd Bakken of Cambridge, who deserved to pat himself on the back for one-shotting the 230-yard 13th at Lake Ripley CC, noted, "In the history of the club (roughly 75 years), this is only the fifth ace on this hole."

Such boasting is not a Wisconsin thing, by the way. One Bertrand Girard of Quebec said of his October ace, "*Un magnifique coup de wedge frappe ...* " Just guessing, but I believe he struck a magnificent wedge.

More than one happy hacker noted that his hole-in-one was a pain in the pocket. "The bar bill was a bit more than I expected," wrote Dave Sterba of Hillsboro after his June ace at Spring Valley GC. "However, it was worth it." Lance Lovegrove of Clio, Mich., noted that last summer's late-season ace cost him only $30 in the bar, far less than the $200 it cost him for his first hole-in-one on league night a few years earlier. "Whoever came up with that rule," he noted, "should be shot."

But there is little griping on hole-in-one registries. As Jeffery Witterholt of

Wausaukee said in posting his ace at Sundown GC last summer, "Shot in league in front of 16 witnesses. Doesn't get any better than that."

Magnifique, Jeff. *Magnifique.*

Happy 100th to Tuscumbia
and Lac La Belle

July 1996

Only in the peculiar math of golfers can 94 and 117 result in a tie, assuming the mandatory quarrel on the first tee over your opponent's "honest 36" provided the proper matchup.

It's true of courses, too. Tuscumbia CC, which has long claimed to be the state's very oldest, is celebrating its 100th birthday. So is Lac La Belle GC, which makes no such claim.

Lay the confusion on that famous disbeliever, Dr. Victor Kutchin.

Kutchin owned the land in Green Lake where the first holes of what was to become Tuscumbia were laid out in 1893. But like the man who said the Hula Hoop would never sell and the Frisbee would never fly, Kutchin didn't think much of the nascent game's chances of catching on. He refused to sell the course's developers enough land for more holes, and the land that had been given over to fairways reverted to farmland.

The new Tuscumbia was developed three years later, in 1896. The first six holes had tomato cans stuck in the greens for holes but the course was later expanded to 18 holes, a clubhouse was built and Tuscumbia's claim to fame was born, even if the state's "oldest" course is celebrating its centennial the same year as a younger course, and after several others.

"It's always been an argument," said John Geils, who, with his son, Jim, runs the course today. "It was the claim when we purchased it and we just assumed they were right."

The course, which is open to the public, is known for small greens and narrow fairways lined by large and punishing trees. Thus, the name Tuscumbia is said to have come from the Indian word for "war cry." More common today is the cry of despair from someone who just got good wood on the ball. Usually oak.

Some of the earliest members at Lac La Belle, now a private club at the water's edge in Oconomowoc, possessed the most famous names of Milwaukee history – Pabst, Armour, Montgomery Ward. The local paper said the "Country Club of Oconomowoc" was incorporated in 1896 "to promote outdoor amusements" such as tennis and golf, and in its early years it did become a playground and social center for the summer crowd from Chicago, Milwaukee and St. Louis.

The original nine was designed by David Foulis, who designed Chicago CC, and Silas Strohn. Caddies from town made 15 cents for toting bags, though the steamboat that carried them across Lac La Belle to the golf course pier gave them free passage.

A course history prepared for the centennial celebration includes the 1923 defection by members who wanted 18 holes. They disbanded the club and formed what is now the Oconomowoc GC, but Lac La Belle survived the Great Depression with a small membership – dues were a hefty $30 per year – and the grace of a patient banker kept the course open during World War II. After the war the club recovered, a new clubhouse was built and the course expanded to 18 holes.

Some schizophrenia remains, however. Lac La Belle has been variously a golf club, a country club, then a golf club again. "Today, with our latest golf course upgrade, we are back to calling ourselves, the Lac La Belle GC," the history notes. "Who knows what we will be after we re-do the greens? Check the crest on the next golf shirt you buy at the pro shop for any changes in status."

The great part of looking back during centennial years is remembering the old stories, some perhaps improved with time, but worth retelling. At Lac La Belle, that includes the time Mark Paliafito scored a hole-in-one on the par-3 seventh – but only because his shot went wide, hit his mother on the head and bounced into the hole.

Or this one, the time the late Robert Hyack was putting when a bird flew over and dropped him a message.

"Bob looked up, with the message running down his forehead, and said 'For some people, they sing.'"

If true, the tune should be "Happy Birthday."

Author's Note: Lac La Belle CC recently became a daily-fee golf course in Oconomowoc by the name of Rolling Hills CC.

Help is everywhere

May 1993

Hoo boy, this could be trouble. As we speak, I am 24 hours from an airplane that will whisk me off to play golf and 48 hours from the first tee.

And I'm having trouble with the knee kiss at the end of my swing.

Or was it supposed to be hips kiss? I can't remember just now.

No, knees, I'm sure. Funny, isn't it? Until a few days ago that was not even one of the many crises in my life, not like the squirrel that's invaded my garage or looming sin taxes.

Then Johnny Miller came on TV with one of those golfo-mercials and instead of turning away as I would from dirty scenes at the movies, I soaked it up like a bar rag chasing spilled beer.

He said something or other about your shoulder and finishing high and then said, remember, always finish your swing with your knees together, like they are kissing.

I'd never heard it put quite that way before but it sounded good. So when I went to the golf shop and range where I'd taken my clubs for new grips and to have the hook taken out of my driver, I decided to try it out.

Oh, these knobby knees kissed, all right. They puckered up and smushed like a couple of lovestruck sophomores on the basement couch, and I know my finish looked as good as Johnny Miller's.

But for some reason that ball went off the club like a duck drunk on lead shot. It was a pure line drive, about a foot high and aloft for heck, 30, 40 yards if it flew an inch. Off an 8-iron.

I was so busy kissing knees I forgot to put my left knee behind the ball and point my right knee at the target and ... aargh!

Golf is an odd game, but you already know that. In no other sport do players need so much help, but in no other sport are they so easily overmedicated.

Books, videos, commercials, the guy in your foursome you know you are better than but never seem to beat – anybody who's ever made a 4-foot putt is a swing doctor these days. For those of us who are addicts, these experts are at best co-dependents; at worst, pushers.

In the bookstore I favor, there are four full shelves of golf books, of which at least 51 are instructionals. And that doesn't even include Harvey Penick's current best-selling "Little Red Book," which was sold out. Only in golf would a little red book be more in demand than a little black book.

Possibilities for the weak and needy ran from "Golf My Way" to "Golf Your Way," from "Visual Golf" to "Quantum Golf," from Ben Hogan's "Five Lessons" to Jack Nicklaus's "My 55 Ways to Lower Your Golf Score."

Golf, it seems, was 11 times simpler in Hogan's day. It's so complicated today that "How to Master A Great Golf Swing" runs a head-spinning 296 pages of charts and arrows and pictures.

"Swing Thoughts" was a tome, too, a collection of pro swing secrets that ran from Rocco Mediate's "Turn, Turn, Turn" to Ben Crenshaw's duh-inspiring "Swing the Clubhead." Now why didn't I think of that?

For the impatient there was "Power Swing in 15 Days," "Two Putt Greens in 18 Days" and of course, "Correct the Most Common Problems in Golf in 10 Days."

Why not just declare two-putting your most common problem, lick it in 10 days and get started on the power swing early? But what do I know? My favorite instructional is Bob Brue's "Power Shanking," a beautifully bound volume, but with every page as blank as an editor's conscience.

Magazines are full of it, too. Help, I mean. Last month *Golf Digest* offered to teach readers to swing easy and hit big like Fred Couples, strengthen leg action like Nick Faldo, make solid contact like Seve Ballesteros and "tighten your turn like Gary McCord," which sounds to me like Cecil Fielder getting home run tips from Bob Uecker.

It's all too much. So no more knee kisses for me, no sir. When I hit that first tee I am determined to, as Henry David Thoreau, the David Leadbetter of his day, told high handicappers long ago, "Simplify."

No 55 tips from Nicklaus, not even five from Hogan.

Just that one from John Daly, where you stand over the ball, steel yourself for the violence to come and think: "Death!"

Or was it "wound?" Or "hurt?" I can't remember just now.

Author's Note: In re-reading these columns, I find this is the second comparison of "Harvey Penick's Little Red Book" with a black book. And, I hope, the last.

Hit it into the
next state ... for real

September 1999

I started the round with my patented brand of ragged play, but even after three or four early bogeys made their way onto the card I still had hope in my bag.

It'll be different, I kept saying, when I get back to Wisconsin. And on the fifth tee there I was, home sweet home at last. And it was different. I double-bogeyed.

Gateway GC in Land O' Lakes is a golf course for the latent gorilla in all of us, a place for anyone who has ever waggled the big dog menacingly and vowed to hit that ball into the next state.

At Gateway the next state is just across the road. The nine-hole layout's first four holes are on the Michigan side of our state's northern border; the final five are in Wisconsin. And as at certain other borders around the world, this geographic curiosity can be hazardous. One of the players in the foursome in front of me hit a pop-fly shank off the fifth tee, which lies in Wisconsin, and hit the clubhouse next to No. 1.

Those of us still in Michigan ducked for cover.

The course's beginning was as bifurcated as its location. Designed by Robert Bruce Harris, its northern holes were built in 1941. But the war effort required every piece of heavy equipment available, so construction lagged until after the war ended. The Wisconsin holes were then completed and play was underway.

It was known then as King's Gateway, after the Detroit broadcaster named King who owned the club. And it reportedly had its share of notable players.

"I know President Eisenhower used to come up here a lot and play the course," said superintendent Todd Renk, whose family is one of the course's co-owners. "Walter Hagen came up here. I guess he knew Eisenhower pretty well." Now its players are a combination of local residents and summer visitors.

The Renks came to Gateway from Plum Lake GC in Sayner, another fine nine-hole course on a beautiful lakeside location. Renk misses Plum Lake, but said Gateway offered a chance to move into ownership eventually. In the meantime, it also offers the challenge of returning a neglected layout into something approaching its early potential.

When the new owners arrived a few years ago, only tees and greens were irrigated and the best that could be said of the fairways was that they provided a lot of roll. The key was to get it rolling in the right direction.

Now, all fairways are watered as well. "Guys are always complaining about the roll they lost," Renk said, but few were complaining about the water during last summer's drought conditions.

Forward tee boxes are being rebuilt. And they are in the process of renovating bunkers, no small matter given that one of Harris' trademarks was sprawling sand bunkers. But the work is needed. When he arrived, Renk found that previous owners had filled the bunkers by dredging nearby lakebeds, which yielded sand but also dirt and clay and probably decomposed fish.

"I couldn't believe it," Renk said.

What they will have if all goes as planned is a sporty little test of golf in a nice northwoods setting. The Michigan holes have water hazards, while the final five holes are more wooded. In fact, at least in my opinion, the sixth hole could have used a little more logging a few decades back, though those who play the hole down the fairway might disagree. But even beyond the lumber issue I knew I was in northern Wisconsin, because I kept hearing gunshots while I played. It turns out Gateway has a sporting clay range for a neighbor.

(Further evidence that this is up north golf: While playing the Wisconsin holes I noticed a human-sized loon walking on the shoulder of the road carrying a big bunch of balloons and waving at traffic. Really, I did.)

While the majority of holes now call Wisconsin home, that will eventually change. Renk said there are plans for another nine on 75 acres on the course's north side. The plan is to use two small lakes and some wetlands in designing the new nine, though construction won't begin for another two years.

Until then, Gateway will continue making improvements on its one-of-a-kind original nine. If you want to try it, Gateway is on Highway B at U.S. Highway 45, about 20 minutes north of Eagle River.

Hungry for the game again

March 2000

A h, the life of a teaching pro. In summer, sunshine is your ceiling and warm breezes your office walls. Your home is on the range, and it's much the same in winter except that the range is off in tropical Florida or Arizona, somewhere warm and wonderful where winter can't reach.

So much for stereotypes. Now listen to Jerry Dunn, the teaching pro at Madeline Island GC in frozen Lake Superior, describe the two-mile "ice road" that full-time islanders must travel in winter to reach the mainland of Bayfield.

When the air is cold and the ice is hard, no problem, he said, as long as wind-blown snow doesn't hide the road. But when the air warms and the snow on the surface begins to melt, well, that's a whole different putt.

"The bravest of ice travelers will get a little bit nervous when we have to travel on 8 or 10 inches of water on the ice," he said. "You can't see the ice but you have to have faith that there's ice underneath."

In most of Wisconsin, the off-season isn't what it used to be. Winter seems to have lost its bite, and even in February it doesn't take a temperature reading much higher than a good nine-hole score to get the golf juices flowing. But there still are golf settings where weather rules, and few places where that is more true than on an island in frozen Lake Superior.

And the surprising thing is, Dunn doesn't mind a bit.

"Those of us who live in the North have had this long off-season all our lives," Dunn said. "We get used to it and look forward to it."

Winter, he said, is a time to heal injuries and rest the mind. "And to get hungry for the game again. I can't imagine playing golf all year around. I think I would get sick of golf. Maybe when I retire from all my jobs up here I'll think about it, but right now ... I need to get away from it."

All his jobs? On an island with just 150 permanent residents (the summer population swells into the thousands) no one can get by with just one job. Dunn's main business is caring for the houses of summer residents. He serves on the volunteer fire department, is a single father of two boys, writes a golf column for each issue of the *Island Gazette* and plays a battered tuba in the island's wonderful Fourth of July parade. In winter he runs the junior ski racing program at Mt. Ashwabay and in summer teaches junior golf at the Madeline Island course, a fine 18-hole layout that often surprises first-time visitors with its challenges. When his arthritic knees permit, he takes part in senior events and while he is only a part-time teacher at the island course, "I probably teach as many lessons as a lot of PGA pros."

No wonder an off-season is all right.

"It goes pretty well," he said, meaning winter the way it used to be. "I get involved in skiing during the wintertime so that pretty much occupies my mind and keeps me from worrying about when golf starts. The snow is off the driving range on the 10th of April – I know it sounds silly but I can just about plan on that – and that gives me two weeks to hit balls before we can kind of sneak onto the course. But just having snow disappear doesn't mean the frost (is gone). Really, May 1 is about as early as it can be."

His "Swing Thots" column allows him to share whatever is on his "golf mind" once a month or so. In November he usually reviews the season just ended; in December he might invite readers to make a checklist of what works for them on the golf course, then tells them to remember those things all winter. (My own putting mantra – "Hit it square, then don't care" – came from one of his columns.)

But other than that, winter is time away from golf. No swinging clubs in the living room, no indoor driving ranges ("To me, hitting a golf ball means nothing unless you can see it fly," he said. "Not to mention that they're not going to build a golf dome on an island with 150 people on it.") and most of all, no geographical regret.

"That hunger to get out and play really makes it special," he said. "Truthfully, I don't wish I was in Florida or Arizona or Oklahoma."

No kidding. Can you imagine how sloppy their ice roads must get?

Author's Note: Jerry Dunn is retired from teaching golf now, but playing more. Not a bad trade.

Ice is nice, but no match for green thatch

May 1995

I may never play inspired golf, but I have inspired a golf course. That's something.

I got a note a while back from John Pierpont, who lives up north in Mercer, the little town that bills itself as the loon capital of Wisconsin.

It had been a few years. The last time we talked was in 1989 when I joined him for a round of golf one January day on the snow-covered course he built behind his house on frozen Lake Tahoe.

Yes, January. Did I mention the loon aspect?

The idea to build an ice course came to him one day while he was out on the driveway hitting balls across the frozen water. One thing led to another – it usually does – and soon, with the help of equally shack-happy friends and family members, he laid out the first holes. They borrowed a wooden roller, like snowmobile clubs use to groom trails, to tamp down the fairways. They used chicken wire to designate "greens." By adding a dogleg fairway through the channel and around the house to a second lake, he had enough frozen acreage for nine holes.

His cart was a snowmobile. On a good day, if he didn't lose too many shots in the deep snow that was the rough, he could play nine holes in an hour.

It was such fun that I wrote about it for the newspaper (the *Milwaukee Journal Sentinel* – subscriptions are available) that employs me when I'm not playing golf.

"Pierpont is perhaps Mercer's foremost golf course architect," I wrote, "and certainly the most innovative."

Apparently, I created a monster. When he wrote this winter and said he had laid out another course, I thought he meant frozen again. But no, he said when I called, "I built a real golf course – with grass and everything. Yeah, right from the ground up. It's just a little hole in the wall but it's a lot of fun."

Hole in the wall?

"That's," he said, "a figure of speech."

It's still the same old story. "I was sitting here one day," he said, "and I thought maybe I should build myself a real golf course."

Why not? He had enough land around his house and the other one kept melting. So he bought himself an old Caterpillar bulldozer and went to work, following the stump lines much like early loggers must have.

Pete Dye, he wasn't.

"When you're given a piece of land and start looking at it, there aren't a lot of ways to do it," he said. "And of course, I had swamps and woods."

Clearing the land was bull work, not his favorite pursuit.

Then one day when he was hacking away at brush piles, a blessing named Don Grapentine showed up out of nowhere.

"Here comes this guy walking across the street with this chain saw in his hand and he just dived into one of those brush piles," Pierpont said. "And eight hours later, there wasn't much left of it.

"He's just a workaholic. He's not like me; I'm kind of lazy. When it came down to raking and hand cutting, he was a blessing. I like the mowing part best. You can sit on a piece of equipment and do that."

One day they drove over to St. Germain to see the new course under construction there, a municipal layout that cost $1.25 million.

"Here's all this big earth moving stuff and fancy equipment," he said. "And I said, 'Grapentine, look at all this earth moving equipment and all I got is you. And I wouldn't trade.'"

The first year they cleared the land. The second they put in irrigation and built a clubhouse. The third year they seeded everything and, "I'll be damned if by that fall it was kind of playable," Pierpont said. "By golly, the next spring the thaw came and the grass looked pretty good. Three years it took us, and it was just the two of us."

He's still making improvements and planning more but Tahoe Lynx, as he called it, opened to the public late last summer. At about 2,600 yards it plays a little shorter than he had hoped but he said some of the holes are "interesting" enough to make up for lack of length. One hole he calls "interesting" has been called the "hole from hell" by some players but he takes that as a compliment.

"You said in your ice article that I was the best golf course architect in Mercer," he said. "This has not changed. This course is far from ordinary.

"Ross Perot said something about a big sucking noise. That's what you get when you hit your ball into one of my swamps."

Maybe he is Pete Dye after all. So check it out. I know I will. To find it, drive north on Highway 51 until you see the big loon.

He'll probably be mowing fairways.

In lieu of ability,
gimme a gimmick

April 1994

They come in the heavy snows of winter, these catalogs filled with promise. When the driveway drifts are still taller than a chin-high putter they pour into the mailbox, the golf equivalent of those seed magazines that so enthrall gardeners or, closer to home, those racy Victoria's Secret brochures that so brighten Valentine's Day.

Not that those keep anything secret, if you know what I mean.

But while they arrive teasingly early, the golf catalogs arrive just in time, as well. About the time the only golf in your life is on TV or in bad jokes (Sample bad joke: How do you avoid a wicked slice? Answer: Let Lorena Bobbitt play through.) you at least can settle back in the old easy chair, pore over the latest breakthrough inventions and dream about pars to come.

Of course, it helps if you have less shame than a politician promising tax relief. Like the Victoria's Secret mailing, some of these golf books are selling a bit of sin, too.

Not on every page, of course.

The one in front of me as I write this offers such conventional devices as never-miss wedges and handy travel bags. It offers rare, old-fashioned persim-mon-headed clubs and such ubiquitous aids as Miss Big Bertha, the favored weapon of golfers like Johnny Miller and me and, as I read recently, of President Bill Clinton and Sen. Russ Feingold.

There are plenty of goofy devices, too. It's as if, to twist that famous cereal commercial, trinket designers have concluded: "Sell it to golfers; they'll buy anything."

Apparently, they will.

There is Little Dipper, a plastic device you attach to your club (presumably not one of the never-miss wedges) to pluck errant balls from the drink. Only $6.95.

There is the Stroke Master you strap on your driver to determine "exactly how much clubhead speed you are generating."

What this number would tell the average golfer who is more familiar with a duck hook than a birdie isn't clear. But for $19.95 you get a plastic tube to hang on your club and another topic with which to bore friends in the bar.

There is even something called Pocket Gallery, which for just $29.95 will get you a four-button "loud, life-like" noisemaker that will cheer the good shot, moan over the bad and even make "realistic jungle noises" for a shot that finds the woods.

"You'll be the life of your foursome," it says.

That's beautiful. Jungle noises. Who's in the foursome, Bill Murray?

If you really want to be the life of your foursome, keep shopping. Try, say, the Power Tee.

Sure, these little babies will set you back $12.95 a mere dozen, but "the fanatic in Japan who invented Power Tee" must be onto something. Because this tee is cup-shaped and wraps halfway up the side of the ball, the club doesn't touch the ball, only the tee, So, you cannot hook or slice. It's impossible.

Naturally, there's a hitch. It's illegal as heroin in the oval office. But, hey, it works.

There's more. There's this Duffix counterweight anti-hook device (with a simple adjustment it becomes an anti-slice device). Simply snap it onto your club below the grip and rotate so a 6-ounce brass weight will work against whatever is wrong with your swing.

Oh, yeah – "Not approved for USGA sanctioned events," the ad notes.

Same with "LongBall," guaranteed to add 20-25 yards to your drive because it bores through the air like no other.

Why? Perhaps because it is "precisely 4 grams heavier than USGA guidelines ... "

Which makes it precisely as improper as unseemly body noises during an opponent's backswing. But, surely I quibble. In a game this confounding some guys need all the help they can get.

Just so they aren't in my foursome. It's fun shopping but rules are rules. If I ever find myself on the tee with someone playing LongBall off a Power Tee with a Duffix hanging off his driver, I'm going after that guy with Miss Bertha.

I learned that from Tonya Harding's cronies. Never underclub.

Author's Note: If you are confused by the reference to Lorena Bobbitt, ask your father.

Milwaukee's Spivey keeps kids 'on course'

June 1995

As the latest season of "Kids on Course" tees off in Milwaukee this month, Hanc Spivey's dream is on course, too.

Some day off yonder he sees his kids – the ones who not long ago maybe thought the game of golf was as foreign as Croatia or calculus – playing on high school teams, caddying at clubs, even winning Evans Scholarships, riding golf to a good education and beyond.

It's early yet but just as three straight pars hint at a very good round, the first three seasons of "Kids on Course" offer promise. From 55 kids the first year, the program will expand to 75 this summer. There are volunteers who are taking personal interest in the kids' game and Spivey's already got some 10-year-olds "who can really pop it."

Now he has to teach them to persevere. If any game can teach that, this one can.

Before Tiger Woods there was Calvin Peete and before Calvin Peete there was Lee Elder and before Lee ...

Well, there weren't many.

"I can relate to that," said Spivey, "because I've been the only one in the state now for the last four years. I try to show the kids I'm an example of perseverance."

By "only one" he means the only black golf professional in Wisconsin, and probably in most neighboring states. He's the head pro at Milwaukee County's Dretzka Park GC, but when he isn't giving lessons or seeing that the grass hasn't grown too long, he's working to see that the kids in his program are growing.

"Kids on Course" is a free recreational program aimed at central city kids, mostly black, sponsored by Milwaukee County, Milwaukee Public Schools, the Wisconsin Section of the PGA, the Golf Foundation of Wisconsin and Milwaukee Golf Connection. The idea, Spivey said, is to teach kids golf but to teach them where it fits in life as well, to teach concepts like discipline, rules, how practice makes perfect – or at least better – and that black faces on greens don't have to be oddities.

That's why he was encouraged by an unrelated development – the return of golf to Milwaukee's predominantly black North Division High School, where sports beyond basketball have long been ignored. Suddenly, there's a team of kids who can't get enough of it.

"That's one of our goals," said Spivey, "to let them know there are people like us out there (and) let them know anybody can play. It's a game you can play for a lifetime (where) they don't have to have the Nike high tops on."

Level 1 kids, some of whom must take city buses to the course, are just learning the game. Level 2 youths, up to age 17, have shown some ability and are taught more advanced skills – how to work the ball, club distance, rules of the game, etiquette and values. There is "absolutely, positively" no club-throwing, and after matches the golfers must shake hands.

In real life, Spivey said, the kids will be playing with strangers. He wants them to be able to introduce themselves, to communicate, maybe even some-day make the business deals that have been made on golf courses since the first putt was struck. It's a six-week course but members of the Milwaukee Golf Connection, a group of African American golfers, have committed them-selves to an adopt-a-kid program which includes monitoring their games and taking them out for nine holes a week to learn more.

"Follow-up is important," Spivey said, "so after classes are over, they don't quit."

Some might, without encouragement. The kids in the program are, of course, all exposed daily to life's pitfalls and temptations. When Spivey recently sent a letter to all the kids personally, because they don't get much mail, some parents opened the letter first, assuming their child had done something wrong.

"There's some pretty touching stories sometimes," he said. "For me being involved, it makes me feel good. This year the program is being expanded to 75 kids, so that's 75 kids that have less chance of getting down the wrong path."

That's one of the lessons golf can teach. It's possible to save par from the wrong fairway, but it's a heck of a lot easier if you play the hole the way it was meant to be played.

Watch out for the guy
with the Donald Duck
head covers

June 1994

I dle thoughts of a graying golfer waiting too long for the tee to clear, and still waiting for lawmakers to finally pass testing and licensing of all new players ...

Uh, excuse me.

"Hey – hey you on the tee. The other end, sir. Yes, the end with the number and the grooves.

"Hit it with THAT end."

Where was I? Oh, yeah.

I like to golf. I like to play golf a lot – early spring, later fall, a couple of times a week in summer and at least one week in winter if I can get away. I couldn't imagine what too much golf would be. Heaven will have bentgrass and gently sloping greens.

But not long ago I ran into a guy who casually mentioned that last year he played 178 rounds of golf.

Imagine – 178! And most of them in Wisconsin, where if I remember correctly, last winter was harder than a downhill bunker shot with a 3-wood.

I thought about that, a lot, as I drove to work each day. There are 365 days in a year. Winter puts a solid 120 or so out of play. Courses are busy, you can't always get on, and 178 rounds at an average of 4.5 hours (six if he's behind this guy with the Donald Duck head covers in front of me) adds up to an average work year for most people – not to mention the expense involved.

I mean, I thought about it a lot. Next time I saw him I said, "How the heck can you do that?"

"I'm a student," he said.

Ah, of course. As ever, youth is wasted on the young.

Excuse me again.

"Hey, you – the sloped club is for sand traps. You want the flat one. Yes, like ... oh, never mind."

Often the biggest mystery in golf is not how that 40-foot, downhill sidewinder to save double bogey will break, but who are we paired with?

Amazingly, few duds. But any game that has winners also has its challenges. My wife and I were once paired with a guy who swore more, and better, than all the sailors in San Diego on their best day.

I believe swearing is necessary in golf (little known fact: the "Blue Nun" was a golfer), but watching – and hearing – Mr. Potty Mouth putt for a whole round can put you off your own game in a hurry.

On the same note, this spring a threesome I was part of was joined by a single who wanted some action.

Fine. We all like action. Tim and I are equal mid-handicappers, poor Dan is a 36 ("Honest!" as he always says) and the stranger said he was a 10.

Tim and I, I said. You and Dan. Even up.

If this guy was a 10, I am Queen Elizabeth in drag and, I assure you, I look bad in a tiara.

For the first time in his life poor Dan had to carry a partner, and I am here to tell you that partner was heavy. We were suspicious when the guy couldn't get off the first tee, then again when he started throwing clubs, then again when he picked up on one hole and met us on the next tee.

Dan can now say he, an honest 36, beat a 10-handicap. Too bad it was his partner.

Uh, be right back.

"Whoa, great shot, mister. Yes, now you walk up and hit it again. Uh, yes, use another club.

"Sure, any club."

Speaking of partners, last week Tim and I got teamed with a very nice fellow who was a retired Milwaukee police officer of the legendary Chief Harold Breier era. A Chief Breier fan, too, as he quickly made clear.

Now, in real life I am a Milwaukee newspaperman, and when he was chief, the law-and-order (at the very least) Breier didn't have much use for newspapermen. We were the deep fairway bunkers in his life, you might say, the shutter click in his backswing.

As we played on I never found occasion to say what I did for a living but the stories went on until about the 16th hole where our new friend was telling a riotous tale about the day Chief Breier picked up a newspaper reporter by the throat and threw him right out of the office.

"That's great," Tim said with a smirk. "I think they should do that to those !@#$%^&*!% more often."

Funny. I wanted to tell the guy what I did. But I also wanted to putt out on 18 without someone's hands in a death grip around my throat.

I can choke on my own, which I will probably do if the guy in front of me ever clears the red tees.

A mini tour of
that other golf game

January 2004

Sometime in spring, when the snow has disappeared and the temperature is friendly, I plan to make my way to Badger Sports Park in
Appleton, the course that pays tribute to the Packers, Brewers and Bucks.
"You must," it declares on the park's Web site, "putt through our scale repli-
ca of historic Lambeau Field."

That's right, no mere windmill hole will do, and certainly no clown's mouth.
But putt across the green expanse made famous by Bart and Brett, that's pure
genius. No mention whether that is the newly renovated Lambeau Field or
the old place where yesterday's heroes gamboled, but it doesn't matter. Who
wouldn't want to play mini-golf in such a place?

Wait, I hear you thinking. How can someone so attached to the real game
– someone who has played golf from La Costa Resort to the Irish Course,
someone who has played in Ireland and even at St. Andrews (unfortunately,
the one in Mississippi, not Scotland) – be thinking about mini-golf? Is the
winter that long and hard?

Not at all. Let me just tell you three things I've learned about mini-golf:

   1. No less than the Encyclopedia Britannica included mini-golf on its
   most recent list of great inventions, along with oral contraceptives,
   crossword puzzles, Post-it notes, the button and the button hole. (To
   go wildly aside for a moment, the button was invented about 700 B.C.
   by the Greeks and Etruscans, according to the Britannica list, but the

button hole didn't come along until the 13th century in Europe.
Where did they put their buttons for 2000 years? And should it have
taken that long to figure it out?)

2. This just in. As of October 2003, the World Minigolfsport
Federation and the General Association of International Sports
Federations announced that mini-golf is now officially a sport.

3. You can make money at mini-golf.

And not just a little bit. There are multiple tours, from the U.S. ProMiniGolf
Association with its Masters National Championship, U.S. Open and other
prize-money events, to the Professional Putters Association with its $25,000
National Championship, $20,000 World Match Play event and assorted local
competitions.

Even if Nos. 1 and 2 don't impress you, 3 might. If you can make money at
it, how can you be wrong? OK, Heidi Fleiss aside.

The game – excuse me, as of October it's the sport – has come a long way
from the early 1900s when it was called "garden golf" and played with real
putters on real grass. According to one history, bumpers and rails started popping up on mini-golf courses in the 1920s and the playing surface was more
often something hard for smoother rolling. Celebrities drew attention to
mini-golf and by the 1930s there were some 30,000 courses throughout the
country, including 150 on rooftops in New York.

Of course, the stock market crash gave the game a serious case of the yips
but mini-golf survived and continued to prosper as Tom Thumb Golf layouts
added obstacles like water and windmills to make playing more fun.
Eventually mini-golf was franchised and in the last 20 years construction of
courses has become ever more creative, as anyone who has seen the layouts
in Wisconsin Dells, Minocqua, Door County and wherever else tourists flock
can attest. Today mini-golf is part of many golf learning centers, along with
driving ranges, pitching areas and more.

And it's an international phenomenon, not just another example of
Americans with too much leisure time. The World Minigolfsport (one word)
Federation is the world sanctioning body for players, clubs and facilities. (Do
you suppose there are "hot putters" the way there are "hot drivers?" And
where can I get me one?)

The Internet, as it has for every cult or kinky club you can imagine, has been a boon for mini-golfers, bringing news from around the world, introducing like-minded folks to others and making it possible for anyone to be a golf course critic. On the PMGA site, players can post reviews of the courses they've played, like this one about Par-King Skill Miniature Golf in Lincolnshire, Ill.: "The best miniature golf course I've ever been to," wrote Nate. "The Roller Coaster hole is amazing ... "

And don't even get me started on online mini-golf. One game I found sponsored by the makers of Widmer Beer cost me an hour of my life that I'll never get back. Even worse, I shot a 53 for nine holes. And all putts!

So I have work to do, and actually so do you. I checked the player money lists of several organizations and found no one from Wisconsin in the money, though just about every other state east of the Mississippi seemed to be represented. We can do better, and at the same time give new meaning to the phrase "putter around downstairs."

To the basement, then, and bring your putter. It's a great invention. It's a sport. And it pays money.

I believe you're away.

Determination overcomes certain golf 'handicaps'

May 1996

We all have handicaps, we who golf. Some are real, some imagined, but we all have a flying elbow or a racing backswing or an inborn klutziness that means strokes on the first tee. Mine is a congenital inability to stop a graceful draw from thinking it's a hurrying hook, which added to a boneheaded short game is worth double digits.

Then comes Dan Cox, who can lift his pantleg to show the man-made contraption that allows his prosthetic leg to turn, who can play to about a 3 when everything is going right, who says, "I have an artificial limb.

"I don't consider myself handicapped."

By day, Cox is a teaching pro at Milwaukee's Fore Seasons Golf, a remarkable position for someone with an artificial limb. Go there with a sore arm you think is hampering your game and get a lesson in what making adjustments is all about. Not in golf – in life.

But Cox's real mission is to show that golf is a game for everyone. His goal is to get more golfers with disabilities involved in the National Amputee Golf Association and its Wisconsin counterpart.

"The reality is there's a lot of one-handed golfers out there, even amputees, who don't realize there's an organization (for them)," he said. "I've run into probably 10 amputees throughout the winter and say, 'Did you ever play in an amputee golf event?' They say, 'No, I didn't even know there was such a thing.'"

There is, and Cox can tell you all about it.

Cox played other sports on two good legs in high school. But while playing basketball as a senior he suffered a broken leg that, despite appearances, never healed properly. By 1991 he had made the switch from the hotel business to golf, landing a job as an assistant pro at North Hills CC, but the leg was causing serious problems for both his health and his career.

The problem was a staph infection in the bone and resulting complications. One treatment led to another, but none worked.

"It was a procedural type of deal," he said. "You'd have one surgery that would set up the next surgery. You couldn't really approach an employer and say, 'I've got six surgeries scheduled, can you hire me?'"

After two years of that, making the decision to take the leg off wasn't all that hard, he said.

He didn't wear shorts at first, but that passed. Stares go with the territory. He'd stare at the basketball player David Robinson if he saw him, Cox said, so why object if someone stared at the way his Otto Bach Axel Rotator swivels to complete the swing. In fact, that's part of his strategy for spreading the word. He played in Phoenix recently with an amputee, a Vietnam vet, who owned golf stores and played a lot but who hadn't ever heard of Otto Bach's contribution to golf. Get yourself one of these, Cox told him, as helpful as a man with a new magic putter.

Cox worked in a factory for a while after losing his leg but is back in golf full time now. And he competes in amputee tournaments where flights are arranged not according to numerical handicaps, but physical. Those with one arm play each other and so on. While there is a wide range of ability, there are probably 25 amputees in the country who can consistently shoot under 75, he said.

Last fall, Cox placed second in the National Amputee Golf Association Tournament with a three-round total of 220. He was low American but finished nine strokes behind the overall winner, Geoff Nicholas, an Australian who has an Australian PGA card.

The national group has about 4,000 members, though only 400 or so are very active. But Cox finds great potential for the group. There are about 80,000 registered disabled skiers, many of whom would benefit from a golf group that similarly offers support, information and friendly competition.

Golf has to make them welcome, too, however. The Americans with Disabilities Act requires golf courses to be accessible, but the reality, Cox said, is that many are not.

"There's some golf courses that are not very accessible and there's some attitudes that are not very accessible," he said. "But there are adjustments being made. Smart people are making adjustments ... and the people making the adjustments understand there's a broad spectrum playing golf."

Good point. We all have handicaps, but they shouldn't include the people who run golf.

Passion for the game –
some have it, some don't

January 2003

Maybe it exposes a flaw in my own character but the more I get into golf – Yes, my name is Dennis and I'm a golfaholic – the less I understand others who aren't up to their gills in the game as well.

I have a friend who has played golf his entire adult life. We've played together a dozen years now, but every summer it gets harder and harder to get him out. This season he played but twice: once with his father-in-law (the suck-up) and once with me. But that wasn't until early November, and then it was only because we had coupons for a free round.

That's why I like stories about people who are really, really into golf. Here are two of them.

Paul Tabor lived and breathed golf. That's what it said in his obituary.

Sure, a lot of obits mention golf among the deceased's interests, but this was different. For one, when he died in late October, Tabor's obit ran on Page 1 of the *Eau Claire Leader-Telegram*, right out front with the big news of the day.

Tabor's wife Judy told the paper's Dan Lyksett her husband would have enjoyed that.

Why? Because the story of his life was the story of his golf, so much so that the photograph that accompanied the story showed Tabor and his good friend Al Wistrom on windswept links in Scotland.

"The game of golf has seen better players," Wistrom said, "but none more passionate."

Here is passion. Tabor, a labor market analyst for the state of Wisconsin who died of cancer at age 54, played some 9,000 rounds in his lifetime on about 400 courses, his obit said, saving all his scorecards and charting his hole-by-hole results. He and Wistrom had a standing tee time at Lake Hallie GC – the first tee time each Saturday – and through the years traveled twice to Scotland and once to Ireland to try the great old courses, above and beyond sampling what the Midwest had to offer.

"Paul would make all the arrangements, the tee times, do the driving, everything," Wistrom said. "We golfed sunup to sunset, usually 36 holes a day. He always said, 'This isn't the trip to go on if you just want to sit in the bar.'

"Most of those rounds there were just the two of us. We usually played from the tips, always walked when we could, always played by the rules and always putted out every putt. That's the way the game was designed to be played."

His family was first in Tabor's life, Judy said, "but we were really close to golf."

Now that's a man I can understand.

Bill McDonald and Nancy and Johnny Keown are others, not that I have ever met them or ever will. But when it comes to this game we love, I like the cut of their jib.

On Aug. 11, the three – all seniors in their 60s – set off to do what they claim no one had ever done before: play 50 rounds of golf in 50 different states in 50 days. They began in Anchorage, Alaska, with a 5:30 a.m. Sunday tee time, caught a plane to Seattle to pick up their motor home and set off across the 48 continental states. Hawaii would be icing on the cake, the ultimate 19th hole, you might say. And to make a long trip into a short story, I'll tell you in advance they did it.

But it wasn't easy. On Aug. 21 they played Albert Lea CC in our neighbor state to the west in a driving rain. "In the 13th fairway, a mosquito tried to take Johnny's 7-iron from him," they reported on their Web site, www.50x50x50.com. "But Johnny persevered. It was one of the smaller mosquitoes."

That round finished, they drove to Holiday Lodge Golf Resort near Tomah, a self-contained golf course and RV park. "Rain, rain, rain," their account of that day began.

Because the park and driving range were under water, Bill applied the "when in Rome" logic to Wisconsin and made his way to the bar. There, a liquor company salesman was dispensing free samples of a new brand of vodka, and the most convivial host who had been assigned to them by the course owner decided to get into the record books on his own.

"Randy attempted to establish his own marathon record of 50 screwdrivers, in one of the 50 states, in one night." But to once again try to make a long round into a short story, suffice to say they squeezed – maybe squeegeed would work better – their Wisconsin round in and headed to Illinois. And on Sept. 28 – 48 days, nine hours and 57 minutes after they started – they completed their quest.

So maybe I'm a golfaholic but I'm not alone. Those are the stories that make me never want to miss a sunny day, let alone wait until November to collect a free round. And I'll keep this foursome in mind when it comes time for resolutions for 2003.

Life is short.

So point me toward Kansas. I have a tee time.

The answer is:
Plum Lake GC

October 1993

A s the leaves fall and we turn our grip from 5-irons to snow shovels, it's time to close the notebook on another season of deep golf thought I never got around to writing.

A tree, for example, is not and never has been 90 percent air. I wanted to explore that.

I wanted to propose we test and license golfers, not on ability but on speed. Slow play on one Hawaiian course this year led to words, then fisticuffs, then gunshots.

You can't putt with guns blazing. There ought to be a law.

And I wanted to discuss this grand delusion with equipment, in light of a report that for all the billions invested in Berthas and Pings and ultra-Ultras, the average United States Golf Association handicap has changed not a whit since 1980. It was 16.2 then and is 16.2 now.

Though I still want a Bertha.

Enough of that. What I must do here is answer the question I have been asked twice recently, and for which I finally have an answer.

Plum Lake GC.

Oh, yeah, the question was: What's your favorite Wisconsin course?

When first asked I tended to round up the usual suspects. Lawsonia in Green Lake has a wonderful links course filled with bunkers and tradition. Stevens Point CC is a delicious treat, and Blackwolf Run is the best golf money can buy (although it takes a boat full to buy it).

University Ridge is a great new track, the little-known Madeline Island course has stunning surroundings, SentryWorld has flowers that won't quit and Kettle Moraine is the spot for colorful fall golf.

New and grand – and hoity-toity – courses are popping up everywhere, from the Geneva National complex in Lake Geneva to Bishops Bay in Middleton to the Country Club of Wisconsin in Grafton (now Fire Ridge GC), not that I'm likely to play them unless I win the lottery.

Picking a favorite is a tough call. But I've settled on modest little Plum Lake, in modest little Sayner, where once a year, or maybe twice if I'm lucky, I get to play nine holes.

See, I was looking at it all wrong before. To answer the question properly you have to define your terms.

My measure is the best total golf experience. Sure, Lawsonia and Stevens Point CC and Madeline Island GC offer terrific golf, as do many other courses. But for me, Plum Lake has come to mean tradition and friendship and a host of things beyond nice bentgrass.

We play it every August, on vacation. It is the only course anywhere my friend Mike will take his banana drives, which makes his annual round of golf more entertaining than most you'll find on TV.

We walk, of course. We laugh at the pothole green on the par-3 fourth hole, a deep, deep bowl dug well into the earth. We ring the bell on the goat-hilly ninth, just past the deep scar that splits two mounds, the remnant of an old logging road. And we comment every year on the plaque in honor of Frank Hixon, who played there for years and once shot a 27.

Allegedly.

"I said to myself," says Harvey Scholfield, who has been playing there for more than 50 years, "that's an average of three strokes per hole. There's a number of people who believe he might have had a few drinks before he added up that score. There's still some disbelief about that, but he was a good golfer."

The course was built in 1912, mostly by monied people who summered on Plum Lake. Later, the clubhouse, a classic Northwoods log building with the prettiest ring-around-the-cabin porch you'll ever see, was set on the edge of the lake, and no one should play the course without allowing time to repair to the rocking chairs afterward, to tell lies, sip a cold one and stare at a lake as pretty as a dream.

The island you see? That's where Edgar Goodspeed worked on his famous translation of the Bible. Match that, Pete Dye.

"It doesn't have a lot of things that other courses do have," says Scholfield. "But it has a kind of charm that other courses don't have. Why do I like it? I don't know. I play a lot of other courses, too, but Plum Lake always seems like home."

If only once a year, I agree. I wouldn't miss that round for the world.

Heck, I even believe Hixon shot a 27.

Shooting eagles, telling lies

November 2004

I stopped to play a round of late-season golf at Chequamegon Bay GC in Ashland in early October and found the pro shop already closed for the year. Whoa, maybe it was later-season than I thought.

The day was nice, though, and they were happy to take my money in the bar. The course – which I had never played – proved most pleasant on a sunswept, windswept afternoon. But I couldn't help but notice the leaves that covered the greens, and the fact that the ball washers had been put away for the winter as well. After a few nights in the 20s on the shore of Lake Superior, they probably put themselves away.

Sigh. As I write this I'm confident there will be a few more rounds to play on late autumn's good days, short as they are getting, but it is high time to admit the undeniable. By the time most of you read this the season in Wisconsin will be deader than Mussolini, and all there will be to get us through the long winter months will be the memories.

Ouch. Not that snowman on the first hole.

Just the good memories, then. That certainly won't include every shot or even every round but it's what we have to work with.

How do you describe the season just ended without starting with short?

Not in the strictest sense. It started on time – March for the hardy, April for the eager, May or June for the weather wimps – and it lasted into the fall as always. But there were long stretches of wet and cool weather and an unseasonably unwarm summer that interrupted the flow somehow, or maybe it just seemed short to me.

Where does the time go?

See, this was going to be the year. Every year is, true, but this year was really going to be it for me, the year when I would play a lot, take what lessons needed to be taken, get the old swing in order and get the handicap down to, well, who's kidding whom. One digit lower and I would have been ecstatic.

Well, I just checked my Wisconsin State Golf Association postings for the year and guess what – I'm up. I only wish my investments were doing so well.

It was an upside down summer for other reasons, as well. In June I relocated to northern Wisconsin, which meant only one round posted from my old "home course" at Brown Deer. I love the North and my new home course but the move also meant far fewer rounds with my longtime playing partners. Because of work demands (if my boss reads this, what I mean is due to my intense workplace loyalty) I also missed both ends of a dozen-player home-and-home series that I've been part of for many years.

Of several weeklong trips this summer only one included so much as a single round of golf, which is unusual for me. And another casualty of too-little-time was the annual round with three high school classmates, our stripped-down version of a class reunion, the one day a year when a round of golf takes 12 hours – one for breakfast, four for golf, six for telling lies and remembering truths and then one last one for explaining to the wife why a simple round of golf took so much time. Because with good friends it's never just a simple round of golf.

On that note, though, there was a most welcome reconnection. One day late in the season I got an e-mail from an old friend I hadn't seen in years, a man we'll call Jim, because that's his name, who had heard I was in the area and wanted to get together for golf. Great, I said, but first I accepted his invitation to come to a boat landing on Lake Superior's shore where the Native American natural resources agency he runs was launching a new boat that would be blessed in the traditional Indian way.

It was a neat ceremony, run by a tribal elder and spiritual leader who first saw that we were all smudged with burning sage and who then lit a long pipe that he waved in the four directions, calling in the good spirits to bless the boat, those who were on it and even those who had made it, just as the makers of birchbark canoes had done hundreds of years ago. At least, that's what I think he said; not being conversant in his native Ojibwe tongue, I can only go by what others explained. At the end of the ceremony a sacred eagle feather was tied securely to the boat, a signal that it had been blessed.

After that we all retreated to Jim's offices for a feast, again blessed by the spiritual leader who waved a sacred eagle feather over his head and prayed. Before we ate, though, Jim introduced me to the room of maybe 40 people, the majority Native Americans, and said that I was his guest. We go way back, Jim said, and in fact, "I was with Dennis when he shot his first eagle."

And I smiled, weakly, I was told later. I looked through the lingering smoke of burning sage, waited for laughter that didn't come and said, "Ah, he was talking about golf."

That next day was the round in Ashland that began these musings. I played with Jim. I shot no birdies and, even better, no eagles. Sometimes that's not a bad thing.

Author's Note: Jim Schlender died in 2005 after undergoing elective surgery. I told this story again when I wrote his obituary.

Dedicated or deranged?
You make the call

March 2004

Early in January I e-mailed my pal George to see if he wanted to attend a Badgers Basketball game, which is what normal people do in winter.

Sure, he replied, and did I tell you I played golf on Friday? Pitched in for a birdie on nine for a legitimate 45, he said.

That would have been Friday, Jan. 2, a day I spent in northern Wisconsin with snow up to my knees and temperatures in the vicinity of Phil Mickelson's handicap.

Obviously, it was warmer than that and far less snowy in Oregon in southern Wisconsin, where he played at Foxboro GC. But what was impressive was not so much George's play that day (though he seemed mighty impressed by that 45) as that of one of his playing companions, Tom Dehlinger.

That round marked the 34th consecutive month that Dehlinger has played golf in Wisconsin.

Say all you want about global warming. That is, well, what's the word I'm looking for?

"You're following up on the insanity, huh," he said when I called for details. "The guys I play with on a regular basis, we're all a little bit goofy.

"Well, you know George," he added, as if that explained it.

It helped.

But as opposed to Michael Jackson or the guy who married Liza Minelli against all the evidence, there is a good side to goofy. And if it gets you out on the golf course, even in the deep of winter, maybe more of us could use a little of it in our lives.

Dehlinger notes right off the bat that his streak is far from the longest you'll ever find, even in Wisconsin. And given what he has gone through to play during three straight winters, he is quick to bow to anyone whose streak of monthly play exceeds his.

Because, as he put it, "the guys who have got more than 34 months are a lot more deranged than me."

He didn't set out to become a contender for the Iron Man of Wisconsin golf. The streak just happened, that's all. In February of 2001, he and two buddies went to Myrtle Beach to play golf, but when they got home there was no play in March.

They played in April, and while they couldn't know it at the time, the streak was born. They played into the fall; when they were able to squeeze in a round in December they realized they were on a roll and "by the end of 2002 we started to realize that we had something going."

Foxboro, which Dehlinger passes daily on his way to work in Madison from his home in Brooklyn, is one of those courses that leaves the flags up and the door open, in his words, "if you're crazy enough to come out."

"We have our own parameters," he said. "One of them is there has to be some grass showing. We like to hit golf balls, not tennis balls."

And if the green is, say, 80 percent covered with snow, it's an automatic two-putt. But it's more like real golf than most of us experience in winter.

Determination is one explanation for the streak. But so is luck. Dehlinger says the key is watching the weather in winter's coldest month to be ready for any break in the cold and snow that would permit a quick nine. Sometimes that means taking off work for a couple of hours for those two or three hours warm enough to get the job done.

"You get into December, January and February, you're lucky if you have a one-, two-day window. It can be wet and slimy and nasty and stuff like that but we're out there," he said. "We've just been lucky, is what it comes down to."

But even luck runs out eventually. For the first 14 months or so there were four players, until one missed a month and, after the second winter, a second player was unable to go on. That left Dehlinger and Marty Pilger, at least until

Pilger decided to attend the Wisconsin Badgers bowl game in Nashville on New Year's Day and thus missed the Jan. 2 outing. Then it snowed and got cold, and January ran on and ended.

And so there is one. His goal now, Dehlinger said, "is just to keep going as long as I can." (He ran his personal streak to 35 months in late February.)

Because there are others out there even more deranged than he is, what kind of man would he be if he didn't try to catch them?

Author's Note: Tom Dehlinger's month-to-month streak ended at 45 straight, after he passed on playing on Jan. 1, 2005, because it was too wet. He thought it would get better in a day or two. It only got more January, and so his streak drifted away.

Heading for the
south side of 80

April 1999

A teacher with whom I am intimately acquainted has a classroom feature called "Star of the Week," in which an honored student gets to bring to school parents, siblings, pets, hobbies and sometimes, whatever kind of illness is floating around the neighborhood. Last week the young star's hobby was golf, which meant that in the poor teacher's hyperactive foursome of 20 kids, one child was suddenly armed with a live ball and club.

Not good. Before anyone could say "What are we playing for?" an unfortunate swing – a little too inside out, if I had to describe it – had caused a split lip, a bruised forehead and enough tears to sink the Titanic.

I'm going to have a better year than that.

I mean, I might sob occasionally, but my hopes are so much higher.

They always are at this time of year. Normal people assess their sorry lives and make impossible resolutions in January, but golfers in the Upper Midwest – especially those of us who cannot get away in winter to keep the swing oiled – get around to impossible goals in spring when the grass greens up and the sky blues over. The sun outside my window is bright and getting warm and as I prepare to pack the sticks for an early spring trip to kick off the new golf year, I'm feeling pretty good about my game.

Sure, you say, the Brewers always feel good in spring training, and Lamar Alexander thinks he can be president. I get your point, but you can't bring me down. Like Elizabeth Taylor on her way to the altar, I'm looking forward, not back. This time, yes, this time ...

This will be the year I finally break 80.

I know. It's the same goal I carry into every golf season and the fact that I renew it here – in print, yet – shows how elusive a goal it is. I've come tantalizingly close, but that's like saying you almost won the lottery when in fact you were one digit away from having one of the six winning numbers. Last summer, admittedly on a rather benign course, I finished 4-4-4-4-4 on the back nine for an 80. Felt so good I told everybody I met about how good my game was looking, including the guys I played with five days later when I jacked two fairway woods straight over the railroad tracks into the suburbs and staggered home with a score that could have gotten me into Mensa.

This year, no rocket launchers when I least expect them. No missed gimme putts, no shanks for the memories.

Of course, it would have been nice if I'd kept last fall's end-of-season resolution and practiced through the winter. I preach it – go to the dome, swing the club, stay loose because you're not getting any younger, you know – but I don't practice it. Too busy, that's the problem, what with work and watching basketball, and that sore back I suffered picking up the paper off the front steps. But I watched a lot of golf on television and that ought to count for something – as long as I didn't learn anything from all those guys who underchunked critical irons on the 18th hole to lose this year's early tournaments.

That's not going to happen to me, not this year.

I mean, of course it will. I'm not Tiger Woods. I'm not even poor, fired Fluff Cowan. I'm a workaday guy who uses "I just don't get to play enough," as an excuse when what I should admit is, "If I did play enough, I'd just be bad more." Or more bad. Whatever. But this time of year I need no excuses. I haven't hit a bad shot all year, and that's what it takes to shoot the south side of 80.

Oh, yes, it's going to be a good year. I'm going to take my friend Tim even up and clean his clock, even when he's treating me on his course. I'll give poor Dan the 18 or 20 strokes his handicap demands even from a guy like me and I'll still lighten his pension. When I get teamed up with one of those strangers who always wonders, "Would you like a game?" I'll leave him muttering "Who was that masked man?" And when I get together with the old high school crew for our annual day of golf and liar's poker, I'll win at both, on the course with saintly honesty and in the bar with prevarications of presidential proportions. And, of course, I'll break 80.

Yep, I like my game right now. This time, Richard Burton, it's going to work. I know it is.

Author's Note: Lamar Alexander was never elected president. And I have still not broken 80, but this year ...

New course evokes old memories

September 1996

We all have a course that holds special memories. Greg Norman will never forget Augusta National. I can't pass Lake Windsor without remembering my first hole-in-one, how it left me with a bitter-sweet par since I'd put my first shot in the drink.

Agnes Tetzlaff can't pass the spanking new Bristlecone Pines course in Hartland without breaking into tears. It isn't the first course to wet the eyes of people who deserve better, but the odd thing is that Agnes isn't a golfer.

She and her husband merely made their home on this land for 27 years, raised children and grandchildren, milked cows, grew crops, lived and died with the vagaries of the weather and the perverse joys of farming. And now the land they worked and loved is a playground for those whose luxury houses ring the golf course.

"Oh, God, it's beautiful," she said. "It's still a tear-jerker for us because we miss that area."

It is said that Wisconsin is losing farms at the rate of three a day. It only seems like that many new golf courses are springing up, which is good news for those of us who value tee times as much as a good meal. It's terrible news if the alfalfa land that gave way to bentgrass put you out of work.

Actually, Bristlecone Pines holds special memories for me, too, and I've never played it.

In 1984, when my beat was covering agriculture and rural life for *The*

Milwaukee Journal, I spent many a day on the Tetzlaff farm for a series of stories meant to acquaint city folks with the joys and sorrows of a farm family.

I was here in March, farming's meanest month, when a grower is ready to grow but Old Man Winter and Mother Nature are still a couple at odds. I watched Gary Tetzlaff check the window every five minutes to see if spring had arrived, like a golfer checking for sunshine. "He just goes out of his mind because he wants to get out in those fields," Agnes said then.

Just like a golfer.

I was on this land in May, when planting was in full swing, and in July, when the Tetzlaff boys were getting their steers ready for the Waukesha County Fair. The barn where Bristlecone Pines keeps its tractors? I was at the door of that very barn the day a 1,200-pound fair-bound steer bolted for freedom. I was there in mid-summer when the local Lions Club came for its annual chicken dinner, in September when Gary got a break before the hubbub of harvest and again in November for a lavish Thanksgiving when all the work was done.

"It's the same stuff," Gary once said of the seasons and the chores they bring, "just going around and around."

I was also there the day the auctioneer came. Unlike most farmers, the Tetzlaffs had rented the land instead of owning it, and when the owner got a better offer from developers, they had no choice but sell the cows and equipment and move on down the road. Twenty-seven years and they were gone. Lord, it was cold the day they sold the cows.

The Tetzlaff home and barns now house Bristlecone equipment and offices. From where Gary sat, looking out the window for spring, you can see the manicured fairways of the new course. If they couldn't stay on the land, it was at least good that a golf course was part of the project instead of wall-to-wall houses, Agnes said. In her heart – though she would never have the nerve to call and ask – she wished that Gary and the boys might be the first group to tee it up on their old back forty, now the back nine.

"At least go over the land they worked," she said. "(Gary) remembers where we had the animals running and all that. Ron, (her son) said, 'I wonder what they did with that big rock we always had to work around.'"

Maybe it's a hazard, just like before. That would be nice.

It might make them feel better that someone still looks out the window and worries about the weather. Brien Paquette, the pro at Bristlecone Pines, moved here from Florida and arrived in June, when rain was insufferably persistent.

"It rained for three weeks," he said. "I said, 'Oh, man.'"

Just like a farmer.

I told Paquette about the Tetzlaffs, how they had lived here and how I had shared their lives for a year.

"I wonder if they've been by," he said. "I hope they like it."

They do. They think it's beautiful. They cry every time they see it.

A peek at Squeaky's people

September 1993

I t is Saturday at the Greater Milwaukee Open and up the fairway is striding the finest golfer on the 1993 PGA Tour, maybe finest in the world now, the leading money-winner, a four-time champion so far and the biggest "name" in this year's GMO. I am at the fringe of the large gallery, thinking: "What if his voice had finished changing. How different this all would be."

"Nick Price," you say. "His voice changed, didn't it?"

Sure, but it is not Nick Price of whom we speak. And it was not Price of whom anyone around me was speaking when I went out to get the pulse of the people at the GMO.

It was Squeaky Medlen.

"The most famous caddie in America," one man murmured as Himself trudged by, head bobbing like a spring-loaded Packers doll, arm swinging back and forth like a speedskater, back bent down like Price's bag is a burden.

Which, this season, it isn't. With his GMO winnings, Price became the all-time single-season money-winner and a major attraction in golf.

But not the only one. When a youth on the first tee displayed Price's autograph, his dad said, "He calls his caddie 'Squeaky.'"

Along the fairway another man prayed, "I want to hear that Squeaky, that's what I want to hear."

"There's Squeaky," someone said at the third green.

"Yeah, I saw Squeaky," his friend replied.

So it went for the three days I eavesdropped on Price's gallery. Some golf writers sift through numbers for a story, others interview players. I lurk and listen, and what I heard in my lurkings was that folks who wouldn't know David Peoples from Peter Persons knew Jeff Medlen, the most famous Squeaky in America since the one who tried to shoot Gerald Ford.

Kids got Squeaky's autograph. Grown-ups did Squeaky impressions, raising their voices way up here like this.

"You going to retire soon?" someone asked him.

That was Gary Hallberg, a golfer!

Of course, at 10 percent of Price's earnings, Squeaky would be several places ahead of Hallberg on the money list.

"That's him," a man said as that oh-so-distinctive voice squeaked above the din. "The caddie – Squeaky – listen to his voice."

Only in America.

If Squeaky's full wallet is an accident of timing and luck, his fame is the love child of arrested puberty and TV's Gary McCord.

Squeaky burst into public consciousness at the 1991 PGA Championship when Price, his steady employer, went home for the birth of his first child. Squeaky toted instead for a long hitter no one had ever heard of, John Daly. Soon enough everyone knew Daly and the caddie with the funny voice.

When Price and Squeaky won the PGA, the legend was complete. All that was needed was for McCord, the popular, ever-adolescent CBS analyst, to make Squeaky his No. 1 foil, after Ben Wright, and a once-invisible caddie's place in golf was raised to superstar status.

McCord teased him as you would anyone in your junior high school whose voice started to change and then changed its mind.

Would a looper with a deep voice be of any interest? Would a caddie named Ned have such flair?

But a grown man with a funny nickname caught forever on the cusp of puberty – that's entertainment.

"Here comes Squeaky," one man said Saturday, and his friend echoed, "Here comes Squeaky."

"Someday," he said, as if it were Michael Jordan lugging the clubs, "I want to be just like him."

And when Squeaky bobbed and swung by within a few feet of them, they applauded, and one said, "That was for you, Squeak."

This being America, Land of the Free to Criticize, there were some sour notes in my eavesdroppings. One pompous know-it-all was assuring everyone that Price was overrated and had just picked his tournaments well. By implication, then, Squeaky wasn't so hot, either.

And another remarked he had seen Squeaky puffing on a cigarette a hole back, obviously not wearing the mantle of role model well.

But mostly there was awe and reverence, and most of it for that most American of reasons.

"He's squeaking all the way to the bank," one fan said.

Along the rope on the ninth fairway, I overheard a kid in the full embarrassing flower of change, maybe 14 going on 21, all awkwardly crackle-voiced and broken-toned.

"Kid," I wanted to tell him, "don't ever change."

Author's Note: Jeff 'Squeaky' Medlen was diagnosed in the summer of 1996 with leukemia and died the following June.

Taking a run at 50

September 2000

Back in my 30s, when Paul McCartney was still a rock star and not the cover boy for *Modern Maturity* that he was this summer, I was a runner.

Not like Carl Lewis or Edwin Moses or anybody fast. In truth, I was a writer with a day job who needed the exercise, but I fancied myself a runner and lived the pretense as fully as I could. I had a cat named Frank Shorter. I belonged to a running club, ran races on Saturdays, socialized with other runners and, when meeting strangers at parties and other events, invariably ended up talking running with other runners.

Of course, that was predictable. When the conversation moved to fartlek training and 10K times, anyone not absorbed in running would suddenly hear invisible phones ringing and flee the room. But the running boom was music to my ears, so much who I was at the time, that on the very morning of my 40th birthday I entered a 5K race in a small town not far from home, reasoning that I would be the youngest entrant in my new 40-plus age group and therefore couldn't help but finally win a prize.

I was, but I still didn't. A few years ago I gave away most of my race T-shirts.

If I were to identify myself now by my pastimes, I would say I am a golfer.

Again, with disclaimers. I am still a writer with a day job. I don't look at myself in the mirror in the morning and announce, "I am Tiger Woods." I still run for exercise and to maintain a semblance of middle-age fitness, but whenever possible I talk golf, watch golf, play golf. Not long ago a co-worker asked if I owned any piece of clothing that did not represent some golf course and I had to go home and check.

Unless there is a Fruit of the Loom CC somewhere, the answer is yes. But it was close.

So when another milestone inevitably arrived this summer, I reacted as a golfer would. On the morning of my 50th birthday, I teed off at 7 a.m. and didn't hole out my last putt until almost 5 p.m.

Fifty holes later. Fifty on my 50th, on two courses with a wide spit of Lake Superior in between.

And I walked – not ran – every one.

Call it a self-indulgent Boomer thing if you must but I didn't dream it up. I stole the idea, actually, from the golfer Gary McCord and announcer Bryant Gumbel, after seeing a photograph of them playing 50 on their 50th a few years ago. I decided then and there I would do the same and, having announced the plan to close friends and perfect strangers for two years (funny, nongolfers hear invisible phones, too) I had to follow through.

In the long run, or more accurately the long walk, it was easy, if tiring. I planned my marathon round in northern Wisconsin on two courses that are near and dear to my heart. I made a 7 a.m. tee time at Apostle Highlands GC in Bayfield, my favorite spot in Wisconsin, and a 10:30 turn time to play seven holes more.

Then I made a 12:30 tee time across Chequamegon Bay at Madeline Island GC for the back 25. That would allow time for lunch on the ferry and a bit of rest. And when the big day arrived everything went as planned. The weather cooperated, my wife caddied my clubs on her cart and my feet held up fine. I finished the morning half by about 11, made the noon ferry with time to spare and finished in plenty of time for the cocktail hour.

There were some pretty tired swings in my fifth nine, but I rallied on the 50th hole for a semi-respectable 259. There will be time enough on other birthdays to shoot my age.

A funny thing happened while I was so absorbed in my goal. I saw a twosome several holes behind us on Madeline Island playing the ultimate ready golf. They were running their round.

"Too many things to do," one of them said when they caught up. Their only rules were no practice swings and no walking. They would hit, run to the next shot, hit, run, etc. Their first nine took 45 minutes.

That's not the funny thing. The funny thing was, I wasn't at all interested in running along with them.

Maybe I am Tiger Woods.

Totem honors chief's love of Door Peninsula

May 2005

We in the column game like big, round-numbered anniversaries that give old stories new purpose. And nothing wrong with that. Even aside from their principal virtue of inspiration, the reprise of long-buried tales, and long-buried people, allows us to honor the dearly, but deserving, departed.

Take Simon Kahquados, the Indian chief with links to two Wisconsin golf courses, though most – if they know at all – know of only one.

If you are a straight hitter, you might never come to know about Simon Kahquados, whose death 75 years ago gives rise to this remembrance, and who is buried beneath the Memorial Pole between the first and ninth holes at Peninsula GC in Door County.

How he got there is a pretty good yarn. Kahquados was generally described as the last descendant of a long line of Potawatomi chiefs who ruled the Door Peninsula for many years. He was born near Mishicot, in 1851, where his parents were visiting at the time he decided to come alive, though his father's family was originally from the Mink River area of Door County.

His grandmother on his mother's side, by the way, was married to a man known to the whites as Big Foot, who lived on the shores of Lake Geneva in the early 1800s. Today a statue of Big Foot, gazing longingly across the waters he so loved, stands in the park in downtown Fontana, not far from, yes, Big Foot CC, named for Simon's grandfather.

But back to Simon, who grew up hunting and fishing before he entered the lumber business in Michigan's Upper Peninsula. He eventually taught himself to read and write and became a timber cruiser, estimating yields for the lumber companies that employed him for more than 30 years. He later married and had nine children before returning to northern Wisconsin, where he became involved in tribal affairs. He became a leader of his people, arguing for fair treatment of Indians by federal agencies; he even went to Washington to make his case on several occasions.

He never lost his love for Door County, though. In 1927, when he was 76, Chief Simon Kahquados, as he was called in news accounts, went to Peninsula Park to preside over the erection of a 40-foot memorial pole, or totem pole, to honor the Potawatomi who had inhabited the area for so long. He was accompanied by tribal members who performed Indian dances and native games, though it is unlikely golf was one of them. Door County being Door County, the two-day ceremony was scheduled for August, when it was expected that many summer visitors would turn out for the dedication.

In the end, however, Simon Kahquados was victim of the poverty he had sought to eliminate. He died in December 1930, according to a notice in the *Sheboygan Daily Press*, "succumbing to disease in his poor hovel after months of suffering and want. That this old chieftain of the Potawatomis, in poor health, at an advanced age, and unable to work, had to subsist on a pittance of $10 a month is a reproach to the federal government for its failure to give its wards adequate care."

But one of his hopes was obtainable. Simon had asked that he be buried in his beloved Door County, and so arrangements were made, but not until after his body had laid waiting in a morgue in Wabeno for nearly six months. Because Door County being Door County, the burial would not take place until Memorial Day of 1931, when it would be possible for thousands of visitors to attend and, not coincidentally, spend a few dollars. But better weather was also an argument. As the *Sheboygan Daily Press* noted in announcing final plans and urging its readers to attend, "This is a fine time of the year to make such a trip considering that it is 'Cherry Blossom Time' in Door County, and the trees are in full bloom."

The Door County Historical Society, State Conservation Commission, State Historical Society and other agencies were all involved in the burial, as were

Potawatomi leaders who served as pall bearers. Simon was buried with a coat he had worn to Washington and to Madison to lobby for his people, along with a gun, powder, peace pipe, beads, tribal headgear and other traditional possessions.

According to an account compiled by the Potawatomi, a tribal elder visiting the grave in the 1960s was upset that Simon "had been buried in the middle of a golf course." But taking the longer view, Simon had actually been buried in the middle of the place that he had loved best. He deserved at least that happy ending, didn't he?

The original Memorial Pole was replaced in 1970 and restored again in 1994. It's quite possible to play the course and not notice either the pole or the nearby resting place of Simon Kahquados, especially if you are all wrapped up in swing thoughts, but to do so would be to miss one of the great course's most intriguing features. If you should visit in this anniversary year of his death, maybe tip your golf cap to the chief. Because where else will you find a golf course with a local rule that reads, "Take relief from the Totem Pole area on #9 as defined by the rock border"?

Tracking the young Tiger

January 1996

Chuck Williams, a 27-year golfer from Beloit, knew exactly why he chose this year's Greater Milwaukee Open for his first PGA Tour experience.

It was the same reason another African-American had given earlier in the day when he arrived at Brown Deer Park GC for Thursday's opening round.

"I want to see the young phenom," he had said. And who didn't?

Everyone, or so it seemed, wanted to see Tiger Woods in his professional debut, which meant his appearance as a full-time money-chaser boosted GMO attendance in ways that very few older PGA Tour pros could have.

Even Woods was surprised early on Saturday morning when he teed off as a back-in-the-packer and found himself surrounded by a gallery that would be respectable on Sunday afternoon. There may have been some in that crowd who were new to the game of golf, drawn by the lure of the next Nike superstar, but most seemed to be fans of the game who wanted to be on hand for a little taste of history.

And for some, like Williams, a taste of black history. He's been to Rockford pro-ams many times, followed Jim Thorpe one year, Jim Dent another. But he still had a sense that this tournament would be different.

"He's young," he said of Woods, "and he's part black. And he's one of the longest hitters on tour. It's just something different, you know? It's something you want to see with your own eyes."

There was modest irony in Tiger Woods being hailed in Milwaukee as the young man who would finally bring minorities to golf. One is not related to the other, but for all of Milwaukee's reputation as one of America's most segregated cities, the Greater Milwaukee Open has more black champions than perhaps any other PGA Tour event. Lee Elder won in 1978, Calvin Peete in 1979 and 1982 and Thorpe in 1985.

That's four.

"Maybe five," said GMO director Tom Strong on the tournament's pro-am day.

Well, no. Even fairy tales have their limits. Woods walked off the 18th green on Sunday with mere pocket change to show for his debut, his whopping endorsements notwithstanding, but he did confirm for many that he has the potential to forever change golf's lily white country club image.

Tony Terry is the regular caddie for Duffy Waldorf, who played with Woods in Wednesday's pro-am. Terry cringed when a few of Woods' drives sailed 50 yards past Waldorf's best efforts, but he only smiled at what else the "young phenom" will bring to the game.

"I think it's going to open up a lot of doors for us, trying to play the game," said Terry, who played collegiate golf at the traditionally black Fayetteville State and knocked around the mini-tours before realizing there was a world of difference between a college 70 and a professional 65.

He grew up with a father who played golf, he said, but most black kids grow up with images of basketball and football, a point Woods himself made in discussing his interest in increasing minority representation on the golf course. It's one thing that Michael Jordan and other black athletes are playing golf in televised celebrity events, Terry said, but it's quite another for young blacks to see one of their own playing.

"Before," he said, "it was the lawyers and doctors."

"But that's not the future," Woods said later in his first professional press conference. He pledged to use his influence – and considerable resources – to support the National Minority Club Foundation to help kids get the tools and the know-how to play golf. If he sounded a bit naive in suggesting it could be one more avenue for escaping inner-city life, he nonetheless sounded sincere in saying, "You have to show them that there's this sport called golf ... this great sport called golf."

That much is overdue. It's a lot to ask of Woods – Dent won another Senior PGA Tour event the week Tiger turned professional and who noticed that? – but he sounds ready to take on the job.

That big, beautiful number

September 2001

S o, you want to go off for a few days to play some golf with your buddies but your spouse, who has heard this one too many times before, isn't sold.

You did, after all, promise to clean the garage. And the kids, whose names you can't quite come up with at the moment, need you. It doesn't look good. You start to despair. But then you hear the old "Give me one good reason why you should go" and you start to smile like a man with a 1-foot putt for eagle, because that's the opening you've been waiting for.

"I'll do you better than that," you reply, for once in your life on high ground. "I'll give you 207,000 reasons."

And change. And faster than you can say "that's good," you're good to go.

What follows is a true golf story – an oxymoron, I know, and it's true I did come across it in a golf course bar.

But it was verified by a third party who was a witness to the events at hand – though, sadly for his bottom line, from another room – and by a photograph that did not appear to have been manipulated or fraudulently obtained. So you can believe it. I, through giant jealous tears, do.

It involves my friend Chuck Hitt or, as most call him, "that damn Chuck." In July, he and a few brothers and buddies scheduled their annual golf outing to Green Bay, where they had tee times for 12 beginning at 1:30 p.m. Naturally those leaving Milwaukee departed early so as not to be late.

Like, seven hours early, because their first stop was the Oneida Casino, golf being a game without sufficient opportunities to lose money. Once there, several of the party headed off for breakfast, while Chuck and two buddies, Phil Martell and Jeff Liegler, all of Cudahy, went directly to the casino, where they agreed they would first try the Wheel of Fortune game. This did not involve asking Vanna White to fill out their foursome. Apparently it is a quarter slot machine game tied to other Indian casinos across the country, a pooling arrangement that provides for much higher jackpots than your average run-of-the-mill one-armed bandits. Such as – if you haven't already guessed from the excessive foreshadowing – $207,000. And change. The three agreed to invest $20 each and split any winnings three ways. Chuck's first 20 went faster than a downhill 3-footer so he reached for another and – this is the part that pains me to write – that's when that damn Chuck hit for $207,662.12. Jack Nicklaus was in his 40s before he ever sniffed a check that big.

You might be thinking, this is a gambling column, not a golf column, but no. The event went on as scheduled, though it took so long for casino officials to process the paperwork and inspect the machine that Chuck had to call Brown County GC and say, "Could you please move us back an hour? I just won $207,000. And tell my brother to start a tab."

And of course when his brother, who had not been at Oneida, arrived to play at the appointed hour, he did not believe the pro's explanation for the delay.

"Yeah, right. Where is he? In the men's room? Under the counter? Sure, $207,000. Tell me another one." It didn't help further that the casino wanted to withhold some of the winnings because that damn Chuck, who was riding with someone else, had left his wallet and identification at home. You know what he used as evidence of who he was? His Milwaukee County golf card, that's what. Oh, fine, Mr. Hitt. We can trust a golfer. Here's your money.

The jackpot, it will make you feel better to know, melted faster than any of John Daly's marriages. The $207,000 and change was to be paid over 21 years; they elected, instead, to accept about half up front, which after taxes left each of the three somewhere in the neighborhood of $25,000.

And, of course, not all of that made it home. The others in their party wisely suggested the lucky three might pick up the tab for the day, which meant $600 in green fees even before you start calculating 12 thirsts.

But the game went on as planned. And that damn Chuck – "It was a good day," he said later – shot a 78.

Mean, green envy is a terrible thing, one of the seven deadly sins and not becoming in one so mannered as I. But try and avoid it, I can't. Insane jealousy is just a bit of what comes to mind when I sit at home, pondering my own sorry life and thinking of that number.

That big, beautiful number.

I mean, I've never come close to a 78.

Wisconsin is hot for golf course properties

January 2002

I know. You're already scoffing and you haven't even read this. Hey, I was surprised, too.

But a national survey has concluded that, when it comes to choosing a golf home, Wisconsin is a better choice than such famous golf meccas as Phoenix and Tucson, Las Vegas, Lake of the Ozarks and – hold on to your balatas – even Florida.

Oh, and Hawaii, too. Bye-bye, Maui. Hello, Sheboygan.

I hear the snickers and you have a right to be skeptical. By the time you get this magazine it may well be cold and snowy. You likely will be wrapped in swaddling blankets and cursing your winter cold, and the concept of Wisconsin as a golf heaven will be harder to believe than your neighbor's 20 handicap.

On the other hand, as I write this in early December, it is 60 degrees outside, the golf course I played yesterday was filled with players in shorts and shirtsleeves and the beverage cart – a beverage cart in December, for crying out loud! – was in service and selling cold beer. Besides, I found the survey in a magazine and as we in the media always say, you just can't print it if it isn't true.

"Finding Your Golf Home" was prepared jointly by *Golf Digest* and *BusinessWeek* to help the aging and affluent golf population find the "idyllic lifestyle" of golf community living. Four million Americans already live in golf course communities and the number is expected to grow, the magazine said, so how do you find the right 18- or 108-hole neighborhood?

There were tips on investing in a golf community, joining the "right" club, renting versus time-sharing and other topics, but it was the eye-catching "18 Places to Settle Down" that, well, caught my eye.

To identify those places, surveyors divided the U.S. into six macro regions (Florida and Gulf Coast, Great Lakes, Sunbelt, etc.) and then selected three desirable areas in each one, based on availability and caliber of golf facilities. Climate was a major factor – an Oklahoma State University climatologist quantified the number of playable golf days at each location – but such factors as crime, traffic density, health care and housing also were put into the mix. Rankings in each category contributed to a composite score.

Obviously, the sheer number of good golf holes weighed heavily because the single best region was northwest Michigan, which ranked only 14 out of 18 regions for climate but was second in courses per avid golfer and third in quality of golf. Nobody who has visited the Traverse City, Boyne City, Petoskey and Charlevoix areas could argue with that.

Second was the Southern Pines/Chapel Hill area of North Carolina, followed by Hilton Head and Savannah, west central Oregon, the Gulf Coast and northwest Arkansas/southwest Missouri.

Then, in seventh place, came northwest Illinois/southwest Wisconsin (roughly the region from Rockford and Madison west through Galena) and in eighth place was eastern Wisconsin, anchored by the famed courses at Blackwolf Run and Whistling Straits. Phoenix/Tucson came in ninth, Florida showed up at 13, Hawaii grabbed 14 and California 15.

To no one's surprise, our two regions came in 17 and 18 in climate – I'll pause here while you stoke the fire – with but 208 and 210 play days in a year compared to 360 in Hawaii. The quality of golf was another shortcoming; northwest Illinois/southwest Wisconsin ranked 16th on the top 18 list and eastern Wisconsin 14th. We scored so-so for health care but near the top in lack of congestion and housing affordability.

But the bragging rights are all ours where crime is concerned. Northwest Illinois/southwest Wisconsin was rated the fourth-lowest for serious crime and eastern Wisconsin No. 1. Hard to challenge that, too. The only serious crime I could come up with for Sheboygan was the day Pete Dye's dog chased one of Herb Kohler's sheep into Lake Michigan and watched it drown.

On one hand, the survey may have merely proved that, as has been famously said, there are lies, damned lies and statistics. On the other hand, it does give you some comfort while we suffer through January and February, longing for the mud of March when courses will open again. D-d-d-darn it, we've got it g-g-g-good.

Before I go out to shovel the driveway, I would call my friend in Florida and tell him just how good, but I'm sure he's out playing golf.